FLYING OVER
TEN
MINISTRY
HURDLES

Charles and Vicki Lake

WESTBOW
PRESS®
A DIVISION OF THOMAS NELSON
& ZONDERVAN

This book is a work of non-fiction. Unless otherwise noted, the author
and the publisher make no explicit guarantees as to the accuracy of
the information contained in this book and in some cases, names of
people and places have been altered to protect their privacy.

WestBow Press books may be ordered through booksellers or by contacting:

WestBow Press
A Division of Thomas Nelson & Zondervan
1663 Liberty Drive
Bloomington, IN 47403
www.westbowpress.com
844-714-3454

Because of the dynamic nature of the Internet, any web addresses or
links contained in this book may have changed since publication and
may no longer be valid. The views expressed in this work are solely those
of the author and do not necessarily reflect the views of the publisher,
and the publisher hereby disclaims any responsibility for them.

Any people depicted in stock imagery provided by Getty Images are
models, and such images are being used for illustrative purposes only.
Certain stock imagery © Getty Images.

All Scripture quotations, unless otherwise indicated, are taken from the Holy
Bible, New International Version®, NIV®. Copyright ©1973, 1978, 1984, 2011 by
Biblica, Inc.® Used by permission of Zondervan. All rights reserved worldwide.
www.zondervan.com The "NIV" and "New International Version" are trademarks
registered in the United States Patent and Trademark Office by Biblica, Inc.®

Scripture quotations marked (KJV) are taken from
the King James Version of the Bible.

ISBN: 978-1-6642-0201-6 (sc)
ISBN: 978-1-6642-0200-9 (e)

Print information available on the last page.

WestBow Press rev. date: 09/04/2020

Contents

Surrounded by a plethora of Christian resources, we oftentimes find ourselves starving at a spiritual smorgasbord. We fail to feed ourselves while feeding others, ignoring our need for daily nourishment from God's Word. If Jesus deemed it necessary to spend time with his Heavenly Father, how much more should we?

When we learn to give and receive, we are doubly blessed. However, our past, our pride, and our perceptions often hinder us from accepting from those to whom we minister. If Jesus received from others, we can, too.

When we acknowledge our own spiritual struggles, we open the door for others to be transparent with us. If Jesus told his disciples he was "overwhelmed to the point of death" and urged them to pray, we, too, can be vulnerable.

If no two of us have the same fingerprints, no two of us have the same spiritual gift mix. Why should we struggle if we are not eloquent preachers, skilled musicians, comforting counselors, or even award-winning cooks? Paul preached, Barnabas encouraged, and Stephen served, meeting the needs of the Early Church.

Ministry can be lonely. Jesus experienced the desert as well as the blessing of close friends. Did the friends let him down? Did they question his decisions? Did they do stupid things? Did He need them?

If Jesus felt that we could trust everyone in ministry, he would not have warned about "wolves in sheep's clothing." He challenged us to be "shrewd as snakes and innocent as doves." Unfortunately, sometimes trusted family or friends can do the most damage, intentionally or unintentionally, to our ministry and our emotions.

Wounds take time to heal and are not easily forgotten. It is no simple matter. Our only hope is to forgive, maybe 70 times. Christ's example of perfect forgiveness forges the way.

Are our homes "safe, sane sanctuaries" for our families? Jesus set limits on his time and didn't heed everyone's demands. Ministry flounders when it doesn't maintain reasonable boundaries.

Are we eager to impress people with numbers? Do we think we need a big platform to have a voice? Philip walked away from the crowds to minister to one Ethiopian official, a seeker after God.

Have you ever met people in ministry to whom you wanted to shout, "Will you just lighten up a little?" We wonder if they ever laugh at anything, let alone their own mistakes. A giggle here or there goes a long way to make the journey more enjoyable.

Introduction

During a discussion with a well-known politician, who was a member of our church, we were expressing concern over some bad press as he prepared for an election year. His reassuring response was, "It's just politics."

We have followed him throughout his political career as he aspired to higher offices, and we realize that for him, as a Christian, it is a calling. Thus, perhaps it is easier for him to fend off the jabs as political.

Can we, who feel our calling is ministry, also say, "It's just ministry," realizing that sometimes the burdens, burn-out, bashes, and betrayals unfortunately come with the job because we work with imperfect people?

Though ministry is a high calling, we must realize that sometimes we can feel awfully low as we face the hurdles along the way. At one time more than 23 ministry couples attended our church because they were in the process of healing from one or more hurdles that they were not able to overcome at the time.

Our younger daughter ran track in high school and university levels. Thus, we sat many hours watching all the track events because one of her events was the last one of the meets. The hurdles fascinated yet frightened us the most. We observed hurdlers who focused and flew cleanly over every hurdle. Other hurdlers would clip almost every hurdle, even knocking some over, but not disqualify. Those who were disqualified either had two false starts or tried to clear the hurdle with one leg over to the side instead of directly over the hurdle. Of course, those who fell while trying to clear a hurdle would find it difficult to finish the race, especially if injured.

Ministry is much like a hurdle event with one exception. A hurdler can clearly see when approaching a hurdle. Those in ministry might be able to predict a hurdle ahead but are often blindsided.

A hurdle event requires the even distribution of ten hurdles except for the beginning and ending hurdles. We are presenting ten hurdles that people in ministry may encounter. Some are misconceptions and others are devastating mines, but all can be overcome.

Most of the stories we share are true stories with fictional names to protect the privacy of the people involved. Keep in mind that some hurdles may be of our own making, while others are intentionally or unintentionally placed in our race by others, sometimes those we trusted most.

One pastor, Rory, recently wrote to us that he thought about 90% of the challenges in ministry began and ended with him. "The need to turn the volume down on situations and not add on is what God is teaching and prompting me to change in my ministry."

He further wrote, "I look back to the churches I have served and been blessed by. In each one I have found more than enough wounds. Most of my wounds were scratches I dug into wounds. I wish I had seen things that way when I was 25 years old."

Although we would encourage all persons in ministry who are 25 years old and younger to read our book, it is written for all ages and stages in ministry. Whether we have scratches or deep wounds, we need to keep our eyes fixed on the goal and not the hurdles we have to overcome.

At the end of each hurdle chapter are *Helps for Hurdlers* as well as *Discussion Questions for Teammates*, encouraging group and staff discussion among others with whom you minister.

HURDLE 1

Inadequate Spiritual Nourishment - "I already know all that."

James, a young pastor, knew the necessity of spending time alone daily with the Lord in his Word. Being very tech-savvy, he found innumerable ways to connect with God through the internet from daily devotionals to various versions and paraphrases of the Bible through Bible Gateway or other websites. He never had to open the Bible sitting idly on his bookshelf.

One day as James was surfing the internet, a pornographic site popped up that caught his immediate reaction. He tried to exit the site, only to be taken to another site with even more vivid photographs. The more he tried to escape, the worse the sites became.

Instead of reaching to shut down his computer, he lingered long enough to know he didn't really want to leave. He remembered his feelings as a teenager when he would sneak Playboy magazines from his friends into his house and hide them under his mattress; that is, until his mom discovered them one day and ended his teenage affair with pornography.

Yet, his mom was not around now. In fact, he reckoned that no one would know. Satan had put out the bait. He hadn't passed on by but swallowed the bait and was hooked. He momentarily thought of the price to pay, yet the pull was more satisfying.

The next morning he thought he would visit the website for a few seconds, but seconds turned into hours – hours that he was supposed to be spending in sermon preparation.

The following morning, he couldn't resist, and instead of spending time alone with God, he spent time alone with a connection on one of the websites. Deeper and deeper James sank into the sinkhole of pornography. Fortunately, his wife and friends noticed he was no longer the kindhearted, attentive James they once knew. He spent more and more time alone with his computer and cell phone.

His wife became suspicious, found the password to his laptop, and opened it one evening while James was at a meeting. By the time he came home, she had packed his bags and lovingly composed an ultimatum. She told him to ask forgiveness and repent. She also told him to come clean with the elders of the church, submit to counseling, and find men who would hold him accountable. Then she might consider letting him return home. Because of his addiction, he eventually lost his church position and family.

What went wrong? Why have others in ministry succumbed to such moral failures? Some who have failed have responded that they had become lax in their time in the Word of God. Further and further away from the power of the Scriptures and the Holy Spirit leaves one vulnerable to Satan's temptations and moral failure.

Psalm 119:9-11 tells us, "How can a young man keep his way pure? By living according to your word. I seek you with all my heart;

do not let me stray from your commands. I have hidden your word in my heart that I might not sin against you."

A desire for the Word is necessary. Further in Psalm 119, we read in verse 16, "I delight in your decrees; I will not neglect your word."

Grace loved to poke around her local Christian bookstore. She was an experienced leader of the women's ministry of her church and was always on the lookout for useful material. One day Grace paid close attention to Diane, the bookstore owner, who was looking very despondent.

Grace didn't waste time. "What's wrong?" she asked.

Diane sighed. "I'm fighting depression and burnout," she admitted.

"How's your daily quiet time?" Grace questioned.

"Who has time for that? Diane huffed. "I'm too busy selling Bibles and books to others."

Diane had sadly lost her desire and had never truly established a discipline to be in God's Word.

"You are starving at a spiritual smorgasbord," Grace observed.

"I know, but what can I do?" Diane cried.

Before she left the bookstore, Grace challenged Diane to participate in nine weeks of a discipleship course that her husband had written to encourage spiritual growth and energy in his church members. In time, Grace met with Diane and three other people, who had the same hunger to grow spiritually. They studied and applied basic Christian disciplines such as daily quiet time, prayer, Bible study, Scripture memorization, and witnessing.

"Most importantly," Grace says, "they not only read but also applied God's Word to their daily living. Each week they handed in accountability sheets listing the times of their quiet times, what they read in their Bibles, and how they lived it out each day."

Being in the Word daily definitely made a difference in the Christian bookstore owner's life. In fact, she began to encourage others who shopped in her store to make their daily time with the

Lord a top priority. The others in that group say that those nine weeks were some of richest times in their walk with the Lord.

After a full day of ministering to the crowds who followed him, Jesus felt it necessary to spend some early morning time with his Father. (Mark 1:35) Should we do anything less?

Too occupied with promoting the faith to find enough time to spend with God is all too often a situation with which Christian leaders grapple without always understanding the nature of the problem. After all, years spent studying in Bible schools, Christian colleges, and seminaries teach us the ministry vocabulary, how to speak it in interesting ways, what the Bible says about almost everything, and the dos and don'ts of leadership. Armed and ready, right?

Being in ministry doesn't necessarily indicate that we are growing spiritually. When we are not growing, all too often our stamina crumbles, our faith wobbles, our patience frays, and daily challenges become one mountain too many to climb.

Distractions

However, there are all kinds of distractions for those of us in ministry to maintain daily disciplines of spiritual growth. Many feel that we have studied so much in preparation for preaching or teaching that we can forego our own daily quiet time. We think that information is inspiration. We sometimes say, "I already know that."

One pastor named Peter best explained, "As a pastor I found myself experiencing emotional exhaustion. The church I was pastoring was amid relocating and building new facilities. Added to that, I was pursuing a master's degree at a local university and teaching at a Bible college nearby. As a result, I found it difficult to fulfill my responsibilities as a pastor. I was given time to be away. As I look back on what happened, my own daily walk with the Lord was being neglected. I was doing things in my own strength. I was in the Word for sermon preparations and had very brief moments of praying."

Pastor JP says, "Maintaining a daily quiet time is a battle for me. Too often when I'm reading in my personal study, I find myself thinking, 'Man, this would be a great lesson for this group or that meeting. I have to consciously ask myself, 'Is this for me? Or is this for them?' If I don't, I find myself planning and preparing for other people to the detriment of my own walk."

Zechariah's familiar words, "Not by might nor by power, but by my Spirit, says the Lord Almighty" (Zechariah 4:6) jumped off the page when Pastor Kevin read it, seizing his attention. He thought it was a great sermon text and could hardly wait to prepare a sermon, exegeting the verse. Attempts, however, were futile. He laid it aside for a while and later returned to make a second attempt, later a third. In desperation, he cried out to the Lord to give him the wisdom he needed to articulate the message of the passage. After all, the people of his congregation needed to learn the wisdom of those words.

In prayer, the Lord spoke to his heart: "I didn't draw your attention to the passage for your parishioners. I meant it for you. In the rush of things, you have found it easy to do things in your own strength and not in mine. Allowing me to guide and strengthen you will produce far greater results than you can even imagine."

Kevin quickly asked for forgiveness for the times he had ministered in his own strength and failed to seek God's will and enablement. He began to see a change in his ministry almost immediately.

Months later he opened his Sunday morning sermon with these words, "I want to share a passage with you this morning that God has used in my life. I pray, as I do, that God will use it in your life as well." His text was Zechariah 4:6.

Pastor Donny thought he could experience his daily quiet time in the local coffee shop. Talk about distractions! Susan, a missionary mother, thought she could have her daily quiet time while homeschooling her children who truly needed her undivided attention. And Pastor John, pastor of pastoral care for his church, made the frequent mistake of looking at the list of hospitalized members he should visit before sitting down for his quiet time. Let's face it. We can name many more distractions that would be all too personal if we were honest.

Desire

The most honest person in ministry is the one who truly says, "I just don't have a desire to have a daily quiet time. After all, I do study and teach the Word weekly."

Every one of us in ministry should constantly ask the Lord to make us thirsty and hungry for God's Word. Shelby, a dried-up Christian worker, once indicated that when she sincerely and earnestly started begging the Lord to make her thirsty for him and his Word, she found herself anxiously looking forward to her quiet time each day. Philippians 2:13 says, "For it is God who worketh in you both to will and to do of his good pleasure." God does the work to will and gives the strength to satisfy.

Discipline

Twenty-eight per cent of pastors report that they are spiritually undernourished. ("Statistics in Ministry," Pastoral Care, Inc., 2020). We wonder how much the role of discipline has to do with this statistic. Discipline is not setting the alarm or planning the agenda but getting out of bed when the alarm goes off or setting aside time in one's busy day and keeping the schedule. Paul, knowing that godliness would take discipline, in 1 Timothy 4:7b says, "Train yourself to be godly."

We want instant godliness, yet it takes discipline with the Spirit's anointing. Rick, a young pastor, noted that he studied hours for his sermon material but frequently felt like he was wasting time.

Why not just go to a well-known internet website to get his sermon outlines? Convicted, however, he knew that his time spent in the Word had been strictly for studying to gain sermon material. He prayed, "Lord, give me a fresh desire and discipline to spend time with you solely for the purpose to praise you, to seek your will for my life, and to grow in my love for your Word in application to my life alone."

When Rick deliberately and diligently desired the Lord and disciplined himself, his sermon preparation and sermons greatly improved. He didn't need to use anyone else's sermon ideas or outlines. He was in direct communication with the Great Communicator. God knows better than anyone else what Rick's congregation needs to hear and apply.

Still being disciplined, some people in ministry struggle with our applications of God's Word to our lives. We may say, "I read but go away, not gaining anything personally. I always read for others." We might find benefit from using the acrostic P-E-A-C-E in looking for applications for our lives. Look for:

- **P**romises to claim – Kaitlyn read and claimed Psalm 59:16 in her quiet time the night before major surgery. "I will sing of your strength in the morning…"
- **E**xamples to follow or not – Greg gained strength for a major decision from reading about Nehemiah's prayer in Nehemiah 1.
- **A**ttitudes to possess or not possess – Jennifer found strength to overcome her fear of flying when she read Psalm 57:10, "God's faithfulness reaches even to the skies."
- **C**ommands to obey – When frustrated with training a miniature poodle, Patty read, laughed, and took to heart Proverbs 12:10, "The righteous man cares for the needs of his animal."
- **E**nlargement of my thoughts about God – When Debbie found herself mopping up a flooded basement on the

morning that she was to have out-of-town visitors in a few hours, she took comfort in what she had read earlier that morning in Zephaniah 3:17: "The Lord your God is with you…He will take great delight in you; he will quiet you with his love; he will rejoice over you with singing."

People in ministry are often so wrapped up in ministry that we develop a mindset that taking time away from ministry for ourselves would be selfish. That is far from the truth. Amy Carmichael wrote, "The work will never go deeper than we have gone ourselves." Daily we must depend upon God to strengthen, guide, and comfort as we faithfully minister to others.

Helps for Hurdlers

1. Memorize Philippians 2:13. Pray that God will give you the desire to be disciplined.
2. Establish a time and place to spend time alone with God daily. Plan a reading program to read through God's Word.
3. Plan for a retreat of extended time – a few hours, a day, or a week. Try variety with your quiet time. For example, read from a hymnbook as well as the Bible; read from different versions and paraphrases; use a recommended devotional book, but don't let it become a crutch; try journaling about passages that apply to you. Be sure to write in first person.
4. Look for P-E-A-C-E in the passages that you read.
5. Read for yourself and not for those to whom you minister.

Discussion Questions for Teammates

1. Read the following passages about Mary: Luke 10:38-42, John 11:28-35, and John 12:1-8. In which ones was she a student, a broken soul, or a servant? How do you identify?

2. Share with your colleagues about your own quiet time journey. Be honest.
3. Read Romans 15:14. How might you be "full of goodness, complete in knowledge and competent to instruct one another," especially in a staff situation?
4. Share what kind of system you have used for your personal Bible reading? If anyone has read through the Bible in a year, explain why and how you have done so.
5. Share which devotional books have been meaningful to your spiritual journey. Why?

HURDLE 2

Inability to Receive – "But I'm the giver here."

Vivian surmised that she needed to give all she could to the church members in the start-up church where her husband pastored. Even while pregnant with their second child, she organized a meal for an exceptionally large group after the former mayor's memorial service. Soon after the event, the staff divided the growing church into *flocks* with *shepherd* leaders to more effectively meet the needs of the congregation.

Vivian also enjoyed teaching in the church. When she discipled a group of women during a nine-week course, she humbly asked them to pray that she might find the lost diamond from her wedding ring set, feeling it paled in comparison to others' needs.

Weeks later when Ann, a lady from the discipleship class, asked if she had found the diamond, Vivian shared that she had given up. Ann quickly responded, "I continue to pray. God knows where that diamond is."

Months later Vivian was forced to be a receiver as she watched others care for her young children and home while she recuperated from major surgery. After Ann and her sister-in-law helped one day, Ann stayed for a few minutes longer.

"Do you have any particular cleaning request?" she asked.

"Well," Vivian replied, "my little kitchen floor is sticky and could use a thorough mopping."

When Ann asked for a scrub brush, Vivian mused, "It can't be that bad."

However, she simply gave her a brush and left the room. A few minutes later Vivian heard Ann's faint scream. Fearing Ann had hurt herself, Vivian rounded the corner to see Ann standing with cupped hands. Tearfully Ann spoke, "Don't get too excited but I think I may have found your diamond. When I pushed the brush against the stove, the bristles went underneath and flipped it out."

Is it any surprise that God allowed Ann, who faithfully prayed, to be the finder of the little diamond? They stood together, thanking the Lord for the found gem. They also thanked the Lord for the gem of giving others joy by allowing them to serve us. After Ann found the diamond, Vivian looked for her beaming face in the choir every Sunday morning. She thanked God for Ann's faith.

Jesus allowed others to minister to him. He asked a Samaritan woman to give him a drink of water, sparking his ministry among a whole town. He found refuge in the home of Lazarus, Mary, and Martha. (Luke 10:38-42; John 12:1-8) He allowed Mary to wash his feet with costly perfume and her hair. He borrowed a donkey for his ride into Jerusalem. (Matthew 21:1-3; Mark 11:1-8; Luke 19:28-35) He asked the disciples to pray with him in the Garden. (Matthew 26:36-38; Mark 14:32-34; Luke 22:39-41)

Why is it then so hard for us to allow others to minister to us? There are three possibilities: our past, our pride, and our perceptions.

Our Past

When we have seen those in ministry always giving, especially when we were children, we begin to think that ministering only involves giving. No one really taught us how to graciously receive.

Joan grew up in a church family that personified giving. She could not begin to count the number of times she helped her mom cart food to a needy family. She remembered reading books in the church's sanctuary on Saturday afternoons while her mom placed beautiful flowers to prepare the sanctuary for Sunday worship. Her mom also taught elementary Sunday School and directed Vacation Bible School. Her dad served as Sunday School Superintendent and chief mechanic for any pastor's or missionary's vehicle needing service or repairs. And that is just what she can remember.

However, Joan learned a valuable lesson that most children do not experience. She intently recalls the church reaching out to her family when her mom almost died. Her four-month hospital stay allowed Joan's family to receive. Even though Joan knew in her heart that ministry involves *give and take*, she had to learn firsthand that receiving allows others to give.

Mike, an associate pastor, remembers driving toward the church on a Monday morning after getting the rest of his children on the bus for school. Melissa, his wife, had taken Kylie to the hospital the night before when her breathing became extremely fast. He still remembers the spot on the road where Melissa called and said, "You probably should change course and come to the hospital instead of going to the church office. They're admitting her to the Pediatric Intensive Care Unit."

Mike met one of those slow-motion types of moments in his life. That was the first day of six weeks of hospital life for them, and it was tough because Kylie was obviously extremely sick. Everything changed about their ministry lives, as well. No longer were they the ones popping in for a fifteen-minute visit to someone in the hospital.

People were kind to take a few minutes to visit, but when they left, their lives carried on as normal.

Mike shared, "It was really difficult for us in those first couple of weeks, honestly, to accept the ministry of care rather than giving the ministry of care. We had a few different visitation pastors in the church where we served at the time, and Pastor Don was the one who spent the most time with us in those weeks. Melissa, being a nurse, tended to spend the nights at the hospital with Kylie and I stayed home with the other children. Oftentimes, when I finally made it to the hospital in the mornings, Don had beat me to the hospital and he would be sitting in the lobby with Melissa over a cup of coffee. He sat with us for many hours, just listening to two panicked parents repeat stories. At one point when I shared how hard it was to be the one on this side of the bed, he came around to my side of the bed, put his arm around me saying, 'You just have to let us care for you this time, Mike. You do not get to give, just receive.'"

His impacting words have affected Mike and Melissa throughout their ministry career.

Our Pride

Unfortunately, for a few people ministry becomes a matter of pride when we develop an attitude of "You need me and what I can offer, but no thank you, I can take care of my own needs. I don't need you." Ministering to others, then, shows others just how wonderful we are. However, when Jesus stooped to wash the disciples' feet, he taught them that receiving may teach us humility.

Before Kara and her husband were married, he was the youth director for a world-wide missionary organization. After they were engaged, he asked her to accompany and counsel a group of teenagers going to minister for a week in Haiti. She was so excited to go because her heart had always leaned towards missions, or so she thought.

When the group arrived in Haiti, missionaries and medical personnel near Cap Haitian invited them to climb a nearby mountain to conduct a church service. After the service, the teens spread throughout the village to share their witnesses for Christ while the nurses conducted a medical clinic at the small church.

Kara could not wait to go into the village with the teens. However, the nurses asked her to stay at the church and help them.

"Okay," she thought, "I already know what I want to do. They have set up a little pharmacy where pills are to be distributed. That will be my assignment. After all, did I really want to get too close to these people?"

God had other lessons for her to learn. The nurses placed Kara and some supplies in a little back room with a dirt floor, asking that she might clean some of the sores of the people.

"Oh, no," Kara thought, "not me. What an awful job!"

However, a little voice in her mind reminded her of Philippians 4:13, "I can do all things through Christ who strengthens me."

She anxiously waited for her first patient. A lady with an open wound from her knee to her ankle walked through the door. She didn't speak any English and Kara didn't know Creole. Quietness shouted in the stillness of that little back room. She sat on the stool and Kara knelt at her feet. She quickly recalled the somber evening when Jesus washed the disciples' feet.

"Oh, Jesus, help me," she prayed.

At that moment Kara realized that not all ministry is glamorous, and sometimes we don't always get to do the jobs that we want. We get put in a back room and wash feet. However, she never wants to forget the peace of that precious moment with that dear Haitian lady. God humbled her on the spot.

As Kara cleaned her wound, she would occasionally glance into the Haitian woman's deep-set brown eyes. Kara carefully placed the ointment and bandages the nurses gave her. Without saying a word, the woman stood to her feet and tenderly wrapped her arms around Kara.

"I felt as if the Lord himself were hugging me," Kara shared through her tears.

That day she also cared for a baby who was covered with sores. His father handed him to Kara, hoping that she could do something to help his child. Kara later found out that the father had just moments before prayed to invite Jesus into his life, and she was the first privileged person to care for his daughter.

Kara realized on the mountaintop in Haiti that ministry is not only giving, but also giving with the right attitude – a receiving attitude. She gained so much more from those that she ministered to that day.

Our Perception

When we minister to others, our perception is so important. Many who make pastoral calls on extremely sick and sometimes dying people often wonder what in the world we can say to encourage the sick. However, we often come away more blessed because the sick person has ministered to us. Those of us in ministry to others have so much to learn.

Giving and receiving involves so many emotions. Imogene, a missionary to South Korea, related an event that forever changed her perception of giving and receiving. She and fellow missionaries had reached out to minister among the orphanages following the Korean War. One Korean widow who also frequented one particular orphanage found refuge and comfort among the children. She owned virtually nothing and prayed for her daily sustenance. However, one day she brought a small wrapped gift to Imogene.

"Oh, please, you mustn't. Please keep the gift. You need the money," Imogene quickly insisted.

"But you don't understand," the Korean woman replied. "You are the first friend I've ever had in my life to give a gift to."

Ouch! How many people need us to be involved enough in their lives that they might be able to give us a gift? Even though Scripture says, "It is more blessed to give than receive," it is still blessed to receive. Our receiving allows another person's giving. When we learn to give and receive, we are doubly blessed.

Helps for Hurdlers

1. Pray for a humble spirit.
2. Look for the "dirty jobs" to do and not avoid.
3. Share a personal prayer request with someone in whom you have confidence.
4. Instill to those to whom you minister through Scripture, the need to receive.
5. Do a biblical character study of a person of your choice, recognizing times when he or she accepted others' ministry. (Suggestions: Moses, Mary, Paul)

Discussion Questions for Teammates

1. Read again the story of Jesus and his disciples in the Garden of Gethsemane on the night of Jesus' betrayal and denial. Why do you think Jesus asked the disciples to pray with him? (Matthew 26:36-38, Mark 14:32-34, and Luke 22:39-41)
2. Why were the disciples so slow in realizing their need to pray with Jesus? The Mark passage says, "…they didn't have a plausible excuse." However, the Luke passage says, "…they were drugged with grief."
3. Why, if so, is it hard for you to allow others to minister to you? Could it be "the past, pride, or perception?"
4. Share a specific time when someone to whom you ministered blessed you more than you blessed him or her.
5. Which picture of ministry remains prominent in your mind and heart?

HURDLE 3

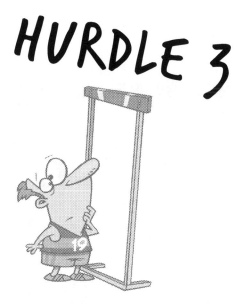

Insufficient Transparency – "Do they really need to know?"

In his early years of pastoral ministry, Josh relied greatly on the counsel of his mentor, an older pastor with a strong record of accomplishment. "When preaching, it doesn't hurt to be vulnerable with your congregation," his mentor counseled him. The next time he preached he thought he would try it. Confronting an issue that he believed many of his congregation wrestled with, he acknowledged that he, too, occasionally dealt with the same issue and thought it to be a significant battlefield in his life.

Upon leaving the church that morning, the chairman of his elders told him he would be calling him before the day was over. "I don't ever want to hear you do that again. Our parishioners expect more of their pastor. You never should have mentioned that in your sermon. You should have won that battle long before you got into the ministry," admonished his chairman. Josh couldn't wait to share his experience with his mentor.

Josh was further confused when a couple of parishioners commented to him that his being vulnerable really helped them as they had felt they were the only persons in the world that experienced that struggle. "Your sharing certainly increased your credibility with me," one man in his congregation relayed.

One could make a strong argument for "not airing your dirty linen in public" but, at the same time, a strong argument could be made for not creating an "image of perfection."

Ministry can be a lonely battle if we don't have someone with whom to share. At times we feel like crying out, "I'm hurting and just need someone to listen." Jesus' closeness to Peter, James, and John allowed him to share his moments of greatest suffering. He didn't want to bear the burden alone.

"And he took Peter and the two sons of Zebedee along with him and he began to be sorrowful and troubled. Then he said to them, "My soul is overwhelmed with sorrow to the point of death. Stay here and keep watch with me." (Matthew 26:37-38)

How does one discerningly know what, when, and where to share? There are some areas in the church or Christian organization where transparency is not optional, such as the way money is handled. Proper handling and reporting of financial matters is essential.

The pastor, however, would do well to leave those matters to the lay leadership of the church. In II Cor. 8:20-21 Paul says, "We want to avoid any criticism of the way we administer this liberal gift. For we are taking pains to do what is right not only in the eyes of the Lord but also in the eyes of men."

One retired pastor related how pleased he was that in all his years of ministry, he never had to deal with this hurdle. Thus, he was never accused of any problem regarding finances because he never allowed himself to be involved in those matters. The laymen to whom those responsibilities were delegated handled them with outstanding expertise.

Missionaries, especially, need to discern what to share with our financial and prayer supporters. How much should we air our frustrations and fears, if any? Will financial supporters withdraw their support?

Trevor and Brooke were rearing their four beautiful children in a small midwestern town where Trevor pastored a rural church. They felt strongly called to go to a South American country as missionaries. As the personnel director for the mission organization they applied to received their references, he was astounded by one response, which read, "If there were ever a man like Jesus Christ who walked the streets of our town, it would be Trevor." Could there be any higher recommendation?

As Trevor and Brooke went through the process of application, received an assignment, and raised support, their four children seemed to be excited, too. However, as soon as the family settled into language school in a Central American country, the oldest son, Austin, rebelled. They thought about returning home to the States but decided that they should share their concerns for Austin with their supporters. They believed that if they were transparent, everyone would pray.

As their constituents and people at the mission headquarters received word about Austin's behavior, they began to pray earnestly. God didn't answer the prayers immediately, but he did in time. As Austin surrendered his life to God's will for him and his family, he slowly became a vital part of the family's ministry in South America.

What if they had returned home to the States? What if Austin had to live with the guilt of causing his family to leave language school and the future mission assignment? What if they had not asked for prayer? When making important decisions regarding ministry and family, we need to pray to discern how and what we share. God can work as a result of our transparency.

Jennifer, a pastor's wife, shared in a Sunday evening gathering how God had comforted her when she had flown to a recent out-of-state speaking engagement. When her fear of flying was ruining her thoughts before the trip, God gave her Psalm 57:10, "God's faithfulness reaches even to the skies." He gave her peace in the middle of a very rough flight.

After Jennifer shared, Rachel, a young mom in the church, called her the next morning, "Since you shared your fear last night, can I share my fear right now?"

"Of course, you can," replied Jennifer.

"I am expecting twins and am concerned that I might fail as a mom," Rachel cried.

Because Jennifer had been transparent, a young mom began to experience peace and joy in innumerable ways.

Another pastor's wife, Jan, who began to disciple a new group of women in her church, explained how the women would be accountable to her for nine weeks of daily quiet time. Feeling her need to be transparent with the group, Jan also asked them to pray that she might find the desire and discipline to exercise.

Irene took her challenge to pray for Jan seriously and put practicality and provision to her prayers. She showed up the next morning at Jan's front door with an exercise chart, mini trampoline, and CD in her arms. Jan was surprised to find Irene had designed nine weeks of exercise using the mini trampoline and listening to the music on the CD. Jan laughed but Irene was very serious. She smiled and said, "Don't you expect me to be accountable to you for my daily quiet time if you aren't accountable to me for your exercise!"

Jan's transparency, with Irene's response, transformed Jan physically as she eventually ran a half-marathon a few months later.

Like Trevor, Brooke, Jennifer, and Jan, we can learn to be more transparent when we realize the causes and benefits of doing so. Three needs exist: the need to prove our personhood; the need to permit parishioners to be transparent; and the need to point to the perfection of Jesus as our goal at the finish line.

However, cautions also exist. We must be careful about what

we share regarding past and present failures and pain in difficulties. Sharing too many details can be embarrassing to listeners. Stan, an associate pastor for a large church, had overcome moral failures in his past and was transformed through God's grace and mercy. Frequently, he began to share about his past life of alcoholism and an adulterous affair that almost wrecked his marriage. Though he meant well and wanted to be transparent, he could have spared some of the details. The congregation and his own children began expressing their uncomfortableness with his sharing, especially when other children were present.

Thus, we must be careful about what, with whom, and where we share. Is it appropriate, if children, are present? Would it be better shared with a trusted friend or prayer partner? We need to earnestly pray about what, when, and where to share appropriately. We must learn to be transparent with discernment.

We question why we should share our weaknesses at all? We're tempted at times to go undercover and not let others see any of our true selves. When we appear as spiritual supermen or superwomen, we dilute people's understanding of our repentance and God's redemption. We must be transparent. By sharing, we create connections with others and point to the power of Christ in our lives.

Helps for Hurdlers

1. Evaluate yourself to see if you are too closed off and want to emit an air of super Christian. On the other hand, you might realize that you are too transparent, especially on Facebook or Instagram, where people often inappropriately vent.

2. Pray about being open and transparent with those to whom and with whom you minister. Begin by sharing a personal prayer request.

3. Begin to listen with your "heart" when others share their stories.
4. List the value of transparency and openness in your own spiritual journey.
5. Work at being honest the next time someone asks you how you are doing. You might be surprised at the response.

Discussion Questions for Teammates

1. Read Ezekiel 24:15-24. Ezekiel's wife died and God told him not to mourn. So much for not being transparent. Evaluate the story. What was God's purpose?
2. When do you think we should or should not be transparent with those to whom we minister?
3. In ministry, how can we respect the privacy of someone else's grief?
4. Galatians 6:2 says, "Bear one another's burdens." Considering transparency, how do you interpret the passage?
5. Share why or why not it is hard for you to be transparent with others.
6. Read Matthew 26:36-38. How was Jesus transparent with his disciples? How might you be more transparent with one another?

HURDLE 4

Overblown Sense of Duty – "They expect me to do it all."

Pastor Roger enjoyed the responsibility of his fast-growing, suburban church. He loved feeling needed and felt called to respond to every gathering, prayer need, sick call, counseling problem, and purchase-runs for the church.

One day he noticed a quiver in his chest and ignored it, knowing he had a far-more-important hospital call to make on one of his deacons. While at the hospital, however, he thought he'd have his quiver checked. He soon discovered that he was on the verge of a stress-related heart problem. With the knowledge of his physical possibilities and not wanting others to know, he tried to slow down but soon ran in the same ruts as before.

One morning a young nurse, Desiree, who was trying to work

full-time as well as care for a husband and two small children, came for a much-needed counseling appointment with Pastor Roger. During the appointment with Desiree, he broke all rules of counseling and began to share with her his stress-related problems. She felt compelled to listen. After all, he was her pastor and she and her young family cared deeply for the pastor and his wife. Even though she felt the counseling session had helped her, she felt obliged to continue weekly sessions. Soon the weekly sessions turned into daily sessions during the weekdays. The daily sessions turned into lunch appointments, and the lunch appointments turned into an emotional attachment of an older pastor with one of his younger members.

Guilty beyond measure, Desiree announced to her husband that she wanted a divorce. When learning further facts, he turned to their young-marrieds class, who quickly went into action. Three of Desiree's closest friends from the class literally sat at her feet, crying and trying to open her eyes to the foolishness of her decision and the disaster that would result.

After admitting her physical and emotional exhaustion, she repented and prayed with her friends. Wanting to save their marriage, her devastated but devoted husband accepted her apology, forgave her, and consented to some biblical counseling by another pastor in the community. Desiree and her husband eventually felt it best to leave the community and moved to another state where their marriage began to flourish.

Pastor Roger admitted his indiscretion and repented, saving his marriage to the love of his life. Swallowing his pride, he submitted to heavy-duty counseling and physical accountability which helped him tremendously. He obviously left the position at his church and eventually moved to another state where he was accepted by another church who was willing not only to listen to him preach but also to hold him accountable for his limited duties as pastor. They had already learned from their previous pastor how to use their spiritual gifts and accept responsibility.

And what about the suburban church he left behind, reeling from and feeling betrayed by his behavior? Could they have seen the situation coming? Could they have volunteered more to share some of his responsibility? Could they have prayed more for their pastor? The questions without substantial answers lingered. However, the lay leadership and remaining staff took over responsibilities until they could find a new pastor. They put a plan in place to protect the new pastor. They sought to help people discover their spiritual gifts to help carry the total load of the church's ministry and outreach. The church survived the crisis and today is a thriving, suburban church with, interestingly, a strong lay-biblical counseling center.

Story after story of stress in the ministry continue. Paula, an editor for a worldwide mission organization, had left her part-time teaching job as an adjunct professor to help the mission organization with its magazine. She committed to working 20 hours a week which soon turned into 40 hours a week with all the demands. The executive team requested her presence at planning meetings, the fledgling staff in the editorial department needed her leadership, the expanding website needed her attention, and missionaries from around the world desired her help with their articles, prayer letters, and video scripts.

One afternoon as Paula sat in her office, she developed a relentless headache. Finding it difficult to concentrate, she called her doctor's office, who wanted to see her immediately. They took her blood pressure, which was dangerously high enough that the doctor, her friend, said, "Don't you stroke out on me!"

Medication soon helped Paula's blood pressure, yet she still faced the ministry pressures. What was she to do? So many depended on her and she loved working for the organization. Praying for discernment, she made a plan to rely more on her associate editor and staff, convey to the executive team that she would not be attending any unnecessary meetings, make a production schedule that fit her personal needs, and teach the missionaries writing skills to accomplish on their own.

Eventually, Paula was able to get off the blood pressure medication. In time, with the Lord's help, she found someone who was even more qualified to replace her.

Putting ministry life in order and not being roasted by responsibilities or severed by the schedule is not easy. One statistic reports that one out of every ten pastors will not retire as a pastor. ("Statistics in the Ministry," Pastoral Care, Inc., 2020) Eliminating causes for burnout could be the first step.

Pride can trip up anyone in ministry and is one of the first ways the devil tempted Eve in the Garden of Eden. "For God knows that when you eat of it, your eyes will be opened, and you will be like God, knowing good and evil." (Genesis 3:15)

How many pastors think we are equipped to really do it all? And we being trained, of course, think we can do it better than the lay people in our congregations. We all know people in ministry who sadly parade like peacocks, enjoying the attention that ministry gives them. Proverbs 16:18 says, "Pride goes before destruction."

Pastors need to learn to eat humble pie. Most criticisms we receive will probably not be for something we did but something we didn't do. Rather than pridefully defend us, we need to say, "I'm sorry I didn't measure up to your expectations. Pray for me that next time I'll do better." Such response will often prevent future criticisms, as well.

Prayerlessness can have detrimental effects for any ministry or Christian organization. Prayer is essential in our lives, especially for those in ministry positions who influence others spiritually. A pastor or leader needs not only to pray for direction but also with his team, regularly turning their eyes to the Lord for discernment and direction. Because 54% of pastors find their role overwhelming ("Statistics in Ministry," Pastoral Care, Inc., 2020), we must pray, pray, pray. Jesus set the example by spending time alone with his Heavenly Father routinely. "But Jesus often withdrew to lonely places and prayed." (Luke 5:16)

Daniel, who had major responsibility in King Darius' kingdom, knew the importance of prayer. "Three times a day he got down on his knees and prayed, giving thanks to his God, just as he had done before." (Daniel 6:10)

Poor plans lead to poor results. We have all observed organizations and churches fail who didn't plan and strategize. If we are called to be pastors or leaders, then we must implement a plan. Delegation is an art that a lot of pastors never learn. Several gifts and assessments tools are available. One church implemented a "Finding Your Fit" ministry assessment as soon as people became members. They soon saw a 33% to 72% increase in their members' involvement in some type of ministry, inside and outside the church walls. They began to make a huge impact on their community.

Jethro made a few suggestions to his overworked, stressed out son-in-law, Moses. "What you are doing is not good. You and these people who come to you will only wear yourselves out. The work is too heavy for you; you cannot handle it alone….select capable men from all the people – men who fear God, trustworthy men who hate dishonest gain – and appoint them as officials over thousands, hundreds, fifties and tens. Have them serve as judges for the people at all times but have them bring every difficult case to you…. That will make your load lighter…Moses listened to his father-in-law and did everything he said." (Exodus 18:17-24)

Setting boundaries should be part of the planning as well. We should set them to give us permission to say, "No." Jesus didn't heal or meet everybody's needs. He had a plan when he didn't respond immediately to Lazarus' sickness.

We can pray, purpose, and plan to carry out our responsibilities in the ministry and accomplish great things in the eyes of the world, but more than anything God wants our attitude. Was Martha not an accomplished hostess in her ministry to others? Yet, Mary, captured the Savior's attention.

Susie was a devoted pastor's wife who worked hard to enhance her husband's ministry, especially as he ministered to younger men pursuing the ministry. Her husband invited a young couple from another state for a weekend visit to expose them to their church's ministry and outreach. After the busy weekend, the two couples unwound over a Sunday evening meal. Susie's husband answered the couple's questions while she met other responsibilities, such as putting their children to bed and cleaning the dishes in the kitchen.

Susie had intended on being a part of the discussion but found herself alone in her kitchen. She could hear discussion and laughter coming from the family room. The more she thought about her dilemma, the angrier she became. The young couple had not offered to help with anything the whole weekend, "Why," she thought, "that dear sister will never be a good pastor's wife."

They might have impressed her husband with their attentiveness to him but not her. No way!

The Lord gently reminded her of the Lord's chiding of Martha for her wrong attitude despite all her accomplishments. Susie asked the Lord to forgive her attitude, put the dirty dishes in the dishwasher, and quietly joined the discussion in the family room.

God wants our hearts more than all that can be accomplished through our hands.

Helps for Hurdlers

1. Check your attitude to see if you think you can do it all. Think of the last time when a job needed to be done and you volunteered rather than delegating it to someone more capable of accomplishing it.
2. Read about Jethro's visit and comments to Moses in Exodus 18:5-27. What precipitated his comments to Moses? How did Moses respond to Jethro's plan?
3. Plan to delegate some of your responsibilities. List the names of people who are capable to handle the responsibilities.
4. Read Jesus' words in Luke 4:18, John 17:4, and Ephesians 4:11-15. After you have prayed, make a purpose statement

for your ministry. Understand that all you are required to do is God's will for you.

5. Realize that your gifts in ministry may be entirely different than someone else's in ministry. Paul preached, Barnabas encouraged, and Stephen served. What are your gifts?

Discussion Questions for Teammates

1. What would you say to a young pastor, who was given three small rural churches for his first assignment? He also was the only one who could play the piano and guitar for worship.
2. Read Acts 6:1-7. What was the plan? What was its purpose? How did it work?
3. Share about a time when someone gave you wise advice for your ministry responsibilities. How did the advice make a difference?
4. Discuss boundaries in ministry. What boundaries are necessary for you and your fellow staff members?
5. Considering your giftedness, how might you, as a staff or team, better delegate to one another or someone outside of your staff or team?
6. Read Matthew 28:19-20 and Acts 1:8. Jesus delegated a huge responsibility to the disciples, which, in turn, has been delegated to us. What difference did Pentecost make in the disciples' challenge to go into all the world with the Gospel message? How can you contribute if you don't feel your gift is evangelism?

HURDLE 5

Rejection of Friendship – "It's too hard to have friends."

The new church plant was growing, and people were excited about relationships that were forming. A few people were anxious to become closer to the young pastor, his wife, and new baby. One lady named Lynda, whose husband was one of the newly appointed elders, closely guarded her friendship with the pastor in a protective, yet biblical way. Their friendship had existed long before the church started.

When people assumed that she had established friendship with the pastor and his wife, they thought they could communicate, even complain, through her to the pastor. Occasionally, the pastor would find someone coming to him with a concern. When they discussed the concern, the church member would tell him, "I came to you because Lynda, saying she practiced Matthew 18, refused to listen when I first went to her. She said that biblically I must talk to you first. She wouldn't listen."

As the pastor smiled, the person further said, "She also said that, furthermore, if I didn't go to you, she would insist on going with me."

Lynda's kind of friendship was one with which the pastor and his wife felt comfortable.

On the other hand, another lady in the church named Cozette, anxious to be friends with the pastor couple volunteered to babysit their new daughter. Family members of the young couple had first babysat the baby before the young couple could call on Cozette. She took it personally and embarrassed the pastor's wife at a small gathering of women with harsh words, "Well, I'm surprised you even brought your precious baby today. After all, you must think we're not good enough to be around her. Excuse me if I don't touch her when she's passed around."

From that point on the pastor's wife could never do anything to satisfy the woman, who eventually left the church in a huff after she yelled at one of the children's workers.

Stats reveal that 70% of pastors do not have someone they consider to be a close friend. Yet, 84% of pastors desire to have fellowship with someone they can trust and confide in. ("Statistics in Ministry," Pastoral Care, Inc., 2020) People in ministry need friendships of trust and honesty. Yet, friendship has taken on new meanings and levels. One person in ministry recently bragged of having more than 3,000 Facebook friends. Because of Facebook and other social platforms, friendship has incurred a different meaning than once thought. Perhaps the 3,000 Facebook friends might better be considered acquaintances.

Wikipedia defines friendship as *a relationship of mutual affection between people. It is a stronger form of interpersonal bond than acquaintance. Some characteristics in stronger bonds include enjoyment of one's company, trust, the ability to be oneself, express one's feelings to others, and make mistakes without fear of judgment from the friend.*

This must be the relationship that the 84% pastors are desiring. People in ministry need friendship of trust and honesty. Yet, we are quick to offer reasons as to why we don't get involved with friendships.

- People will not want to be our friends because of who we are.
- People will want to be our friends for all the wrong reasons.
- People can't be trusted with our transparency.
- People will be possessive, making others in the congregation jealous.
- We are too busy to develop friendships.
- We move frequently and people will forget us and our friendships.

Ian, a youth pastor who transitioned to becoming the administrative pastor, shared his feelings about maintaining friendships in the ministry. Ian's closest friends were once the people who served in ministry with him. But things changed in a big way when he took on his new assignment. One day he was a youth pastor on the same structural level with his coworkers. He went home on a Friday afternoon, enjoyed a weekend with his family, and returned to work at the church on Monday morning. They were still his friends, but the dynamic changed immediately. He had suddenly become their boss.

He would walk into the breakroom where he used to enjoy conversations and the atmosphere would suddenly change. He could no longer enjoy casual conversations around the coffeemaker. He was management to them but not on the same friendship level with the senior pastor, so he felt super alone.

He had not really established friendships with church members, saying, "People in the church didn't fully understand who I was. I often felt as though they looked at me as a wise counselor who could be called upon when needed, but as far as walking through life with us, not so much. I also wasn't sure how to be just a friend to someone in the church. Too often I approached people as another avenue of ministry instead of just someone to do life with."

Pastor Ian needed to know that trusted friendships give people in ministry needed encouragement and affirmation, intellectual and professional stimulation, and an avenue for self-disclosure and accountability. Jesus set an example in his friendships with the inner circle of Peter, James, and John. Three times we see Jesus taking them aside for difficult challenges: he raised Jairus' daughter (Mark 5:37), prayed in Gethsemane (Matthew 26:37), and experienced the Transfiguration on the mountain. (Mark 9:2)

John was also singled out as "the disciple whom Jesus loved," representing a deeper friendship. John was the person to whom Jesus, while on the Cross, entrusted his own mother. (John 19:26)

More than 40 years ago, Charlene asked her pastor's wife, Kim, to lead her through a discipleship course. Kim agreed if Charlene could come to her home when her baby took its nap. Because the nine-week course required participants to choose prayer partners, Charlene and Kim decided to pray together weekly for personal prayer requests. As the weeks progressed Kim felt she could trust Charlene with some of her deepest concerns as a pastor's wife, mother, and growing Christian.

Kim and Charlene are still praying for one another and now, often being in distant states, they phone or text prayer requests. Their prayer sessions now include another long-time friend, Pam. The three could write books about the answers to prayer through all these years. If ever asked about one of her greatest blessings in ministry, Kim would readily answer, "God gave me beautiful and trustworthy friends."

Parishioners, however, would never see the trio of ladies together unless they were on ministry assignments that included one another. The two friends never betrayed Kim's confidences or demanded to be seen with her as the church grew. Often when Kim would be in discussions with other church members, Charlene and Pam would sweetly wave or blow a kiss from a distance. Kim knew she was being prayed for.

However, their friendships were not always serious. Time together often found them in hilariously funny situations, which meant for well-rounded friendships, and reminds us that people in ministry need crazy friends - ones that help them see the frivolity of some situations. They help them laugh at themselves.

The more serious lead pastor, Randy, enjoyed friendship with a youth pastor, Ralph, on his staff that was his opposite in personality. The two of them formed a father-son friendship that caused many in the church to smile. The youth pastor, full of puns, could make Randy laugh when no one else could. Ralph taught Randy to lighten up and Randy taught Ralph to tighten up.

When Ralph assisted at Randy's daughter's wedding, during a more serious moment when Randy was fighting tears to begin his charge to the couple, Ralph pulled out a large white handkerchief and held it over Randy's head. It was the perfect comic relief moment Randy and the attendees needed.

Yes, pastoral friendships come in many forms, yet God provides the right people for the right times if we are willing. One of the most exciting stories about friendship happened when lead pastors at five different churches in the same state committed to meeting and sharing in a retreat-like setting at least once a year, where they could unburden their hearts and encourage one another in their lives and ministries. Through the years they have created a bond that is amazing – so amazing that they were asked to share the story about their friendships in front of 2,000 other ministers at a national gathering.

Forming friendship in ministry can be difficult, yet the advantages far outweigh the disadvantages. In conclusion, we must consider and pray for three things: first, we must *desire* friends; secondly, we must *discern* the friends we will allow in our lives; and thirdly, we must *discipline* ourselves to maintain friendships.

Pastor Randy had not only a young Ralph on his staff but also a loyal Lloyd, who has been his friend for more than 36 years. They served together for almost 25 years. Pastor Randy always feels like he can trust Lloyd. Do they have disagreements? Do they have times of disappointments? Probably. If so, no one knows. They are like David and Jonathon and, even in retirement, often catch up with weekly or bi-weekly phone calls. Their hearts are still bound in ministry, encouraging one another often.

Helps for Hurdlers

1. If you haven't already, take a personality profile test. Be willing to accept and work on where you fall on the scale. If introverted, know that building friendships will take prayer and work. If extroverted, know that not being energized by people alone will take prayer and work.
2. Ask God for discernment in allowing friends in your life and ministry.
3. Beware of jealousy or competitiveness if befriending other pastors.
4. Try to meet routinely with a peer group, even if you have moved to other parts of the country. Not the most ideal of circumstances, however, Facetime and Zoom are available for group meetings on the computers or cell phones.
5. Find a friend or mentor you can trust. Maybe God would have you befriend a pastor of another church. Encourage your spouse to befriend another pastor's wife, as well.

Discussion Questions for Teammates

1. Seventy percent of pastors report not having a close friend. ("Ten Reasons Why Pastors Leave the Ministry" by Jim

Fuller, *Pastoral Care, Inc.*, 2020) Why do you think they don't have close friends?

2. How did Paul and Silas' relationship apply to friendships in ministry you might pursue? (Read Acts 5:22-41, 16:16-40, 2 Corinthians 1:19, and 1 Thessalonians 1:1.)

3. One pastor shared, "Authentic relationships require discernment and courage, hard work and time, vulnerability and trust." Yet, he stated he was a friendless pastor for 20 years. How do you feel about his statement?

4. "There is a fine line between healthy solitude and unhealthy isolation." ("The Friendless Pastor" by Mark Browder, Leadership Journal, March 2014) Express your feelings regarding the statement. If willing, discuss times when you have been in unhealthy isolation. Pray for one another.

5. Share about a friendship with which God has blessed you.

HURDLE 6

Blindsided Trust - "They are Christians. I can trust them."

Things could not have been better at the large, suburban church Don pastored. He delighted in his staff members, especially Phil, a close friend he had brought from another state to serve alongside him. After some time, he added another staff member, a gifted man who had come with high recommendations. However, the new staff member looked for every opportunity he could to pit Don and Phil against each other, even telling Phil that Don was not utilizing Phil's gifts to the fullest. He also began to seek Phil's sympathy and counsel, saying that Don was not treating him fairly – which was not true. The new staff member was simply belligerent towards Don, and he began to whisper in the ear of one of the elders.

The church board, listening to only one side of the story, began to question Don and his ability to run a staff. They decided to put him on a short sabbatical, not even informing the congregation. Younger staff members whom Pastor Don had mentored were forbidden to have any contact with him during that time. However, the two youth pastors left flowers and notes on his front porch. Interestingly, the church board put his friend, Phil, in charge of running the church.

After a few weeks of agony, Don decided to resign. During that time news began to leak out about the new staff member. He had wreaked havoc most of the places where he had served previously, often delighting in pitting people against people. In fact, he had threatened to sue his former place of employment. When that place of employment, a Christian liberal arts university, was confronted about not telling the whole truth about his shenanigans, they simply said, "We thought that if anybody could help this man, it would be Pastor Don."

Instead he almost destroyed Pastor Don, and multiple staff members of the university apologized to Don and encouraged him to hang in there.

After much intense and spirit-led conversation and prayer with Don, the church board made a public apology to Don and his family in front of more than a thousand church members on a Sunday night. They asked him to stay. The new staff member left after several months for another ministry where he lasted only one year. Pastor Don experienced several years of fruitful ministry at the church thereafter.

However, the hurt and betrayal he experienced at that time – even after forgiveness – took its toll in many ways. He often questioned his discernment when it came to making decisions and picking right staff members. And what about his friendship with Phil? Their wives and daughters are close friends today, and although Don and Phil have been together on numerous occasions, their friendship has never been the same. Heartbreaking!

Approximately 40% of pastors report serious conflict with a parishioner at least once in the last year, and 80% of pastors expect conflict within their church. ("Statistics in the Ministry," Pastoral Care, Inc., 2020) How do such things happen? Many in ministry have felt they could trust others because they claim to be Christians. If Jesus felt that we could trust everyone in ministry, he would not have warned about "wolves in sheep's clothing." (Matthew 7:15) He challenged us to be "shrewd as snakes and innocent as doves." (Matthew 10:16) Unfortunately, trusted family, friends, and colleagues often do the most damage to our ministry and our emotions.

The stories of hurt have piled up because ministry personnel, in response to our request for illustrations for the book, sent far more illustrations of hurt than any other topic. Ministry really isn't for wimps. Those who respond to God's call into service often feel unimpeachably right and, therefore, immune from criticism or dissent. But such is not the case. All too often Christians hurt Christians. Ministry can turn sour in the face of false accusations, jealousies, betrayals, abuses, and struggles over differences of opinion. Dare Christian communities reveal that we hurt one another.

John, another pastor, shared about the hurt he had experienced that nearly took him out of the ministry. He had been at the church for several years. He was youth pastor for five years where he'd done a good enough job to be repositioned as the church's first executive pastor. He was uncertain as to what his role meant, but he quickly got his feet grounded and continued to earn the trust of his senior pastor, elders, and fellow staff members.

The senior pastor, David, would leave for several weeks at a time on vacations or ministry trips, leaving John in charge of the large congregation. It was an exciting time and the church was growing. John suspected that his influence and leadership was appreciated by the staff and congregation too much. He thinks he became a threat to Pastor David, and that couldn't be tolerated. After John had served seven years of leadership in that role, Pastor David appeared in his office with a new organizational chart and the phrase, "I think you're really going to like this."

John clearly wouldn't like it since he no longer led anyone on staff other than the custodians. His influence on the staff was done. Three months later, Pastor David sent the year's preaching schedule to the staff team and John's name was the only pastor's name that was absent. His influence on the congregation was done also. Four months after that, as the church was entering the budgeting process for the next year, Pastor David caught John at the coffee maker in the workroom and told him that he'd be reducing John's salary since his role was so much smaller than what it used to be. It was clear to John that he was slowly being made more and more uncomfortable, so he'd remove himself from the staff.

John was foolish enough to believe the elders when they said, "We know this kind of thing has happened in the past with staff members, and we want you to know that we're not going to stick our heads in the sand and watch it happen to you." But whenever Pastor David was around, that is precisely what happened. They knew what was happening but couldn't bring themselves to do anything about it.

On the day John handed in his letter of resignation, the pastor decided that it would be best handled with a two-sentence bullet point in the church's weekly email. The staff heard the message at the same time the congregation did. They waited until Pastor David wasn't around to go to John's office to say goodbye. They presented him with a picture and signed the back of it with well wishes that he hasn't read to this day. The church had no farewell reception or exit interview. He never heard from a single elder. Members of the congregation later said, "We didn't even know you were leaving. Suddenly you were just gone!"

The biggest hurt came in the effect the transition had on John's family. Their son, who was a senior in high school, was trying to decide between being an engineer or going into the ministry. After watching his dad being fried in the ministry, he soon decided that he wanted to be an engineer. John and his wife knew their son would be a fabulous engineer and wonderful layperson in the church. They are proud of him. John just wonders what their son might have done in full-time ministry had it not been for what John walked through.

John spent a few months meeting with a counselor after he left the church. It was debilitating and devasting for him. He tried his hardest to find a non-ministry job somewhere – anywhere. But doors kept closing and the counselor helped put John back together enough to get him to a pastoral position where he is thriving today.

The stories continue. Mary had placed her trust in her new ministry-oriented husband. It could not have been better. She hadn't been so happy in years. The blessings stretched out before her as far as she could see. After several years of widowhood, to then find a loving partner whose life, background, experience, and commitments meshed so neatly with her own was literally a dream come true.

Mary's ministry, besides homemaking and child rearing, had taken place mainly in cross-cultural situations. She had provided clerical assistance for mission administrators, taught English as a form of evangelism, hosted guests, discipled new believers, spoken publicly, written and edited missionary stories.

And then the Lord had sent a new partner to share with her the rest of the journey. Ben had done it all – evangelism, pastoring, teaching, counseling, and social work. He had even spent some years overseas. What could be better?

In less than a year, the bright-colored paint of their marriage began to crack and peel. To Mary's surprise and horror, the perfect Ben carried some secrets, habits, and desires in his life that he'd hidden from his bride.

Mary knew, for instance, that Ben had dated a fellow ministry colleague in the past. He told Mary, however, that the relationship was over. A few months into the marriage, circumstances had revealed that wasn't true. In response to the woman's pleading, Ben had agreed to maintain communication with her. Their relationship had been a compromising one over a span of several years, and neither of them wanted to let the other one go. After a few months Ben also told Mary that he liked to watch pornography when possible and had done so for most of his adult life.

Secrecy, deceit, and Ben's avoidance of honesty and intimacy in his dealings with Mary destroyed her trust and security. She felt belittled and disrespected. Search as she might, she could not find love or even an adequate level of regard that makes marriage work, let alone reconcile her husband's private behavior with his public persona. Ben maintained his wall of protection, never letting remorse, sorrow, or verbalized repentance reach across the gap that widened between them.

Who doesn't know about situations like this one? The famous ones make the evening news and the gossip shows that follow. The less well-known ones can still create a stir that threatens their circles of influence and disillusion many of those who look up to them as spiritual leaders.

But for Mary to marry one, only to discover she'd been deceived and disrespected brought her to the point where she felt as if God had deserted her, allowing her to marry Ben and then wandering off as the truth about their union began to unfold. Here's where the Christian, the called-out, committed leader, cries out in protest to the God who seems to have failed to hide His beloved in "the cleft of the rock." Seminary, graduate school, Bible study groups, and even prayer partners do not adequately prepare one for this kind of hurt.

Mary's broken heart soon became a physical broken heart. She and Ben divorced and she left the state with baggage in hand and heart. Healing came slowly, but after several months of agony, she heard the still, small voice suggesting that she shift her focus and spend some time looking at the Cross. She'd seen that Israeli hill thought to be Golgotha on a trip, so in her imagination she climbed it, found a tuft of tall grass, and sat down. Then she turned her eyes toward the stark, rough, crossed beams that bisected history and changed the world.

"Oh, my Savior," she breathed. "You were rejected, lied to, unloved, and deceived. Even God turned his face away. You asked him why, but he didn't answer. He is the Creator of the world, Redeemer, Healer, and God's beloved son. Yet, he took into himself some of the most painful behavior human beings can dish out." Mary melted a little as she contemplated the Cross. It gave her suffering a wider perspective.

Looking at the Cross can do that. It adjusts our own view of things. Christ's example before us strengthens our spines, even as it relaxes our clenched fists. That tired old question, "What would Jesus do?" suddenly becomes relevant to our own situations.

The ignominy, humiliation, and confusion that Mary felt in the depths of her soul didn't dissolve in a heavenly glow. She did recognize, however, that she was not abandoned as her marriage, world, and trustful expectations crumbled. Just as he promised, God was there. Not as she expected, but there, nonetheless. He was seeing her through. She did need, though, to learn more about how he does that, and her long look at the Cross helped the healing begin. At least, she and Ben are now friends and communicate occasionally.

God does not leave us alone when our trust in others is shattered. The words in Isaiah 43:2-3a reassure us: "When you pass through the waters, I will be with you; and when you pass through the rivers, they will not sweep over you. When you walk through the fire, you will not be burned; the flames will not set you ablaze. For I am the Lord, your God." They tell us that we will pass through overwhelming trouble, but such trouble will not destroy us. How do we know that? Because he said so: "Lo, I am with you always." (Matthew 28:20)

And as far as discernment goes, God knows our needs and desires. How does one in ministry discern correctly? Even when wrong decisions are made, how does one effectively cope with the consequences? We are fallible and we will make mistakes in judgment at times. We must constantly ask the Lord of wisdom to grant wisdom in all our decisions. (James 1:5-6) Those who walked the closest to God in the Bible sometimes made the most foolish mistakes. Take comfort.

Honest conversation and prayer such as Pastor Don and the church board experienced is so important. Yet times exist when not even conversation works, and we are faced with going on and not quitting. When staff relationships and ministry friendships go awry, find comfort in the fact that Jesus' staff questioned him, denied him, and betrayed him. We cannot put our trust in people but in the Lord. Learn the following acrostic on T-R-U-S-T – *Totally Relying on the Unlimited Supply of the Trinity.*

We must rely on the Holy Spirit. The disciples' ministry began to flourish when they received the Holy Spirit. And even when they were depending on the Holy Spirit, relationships sometimes just didn't work out. After all, Paul and Barnabas went their separate ways. Yet, God blessed. One might wonder what their combined ministry would have achieved. Only the Lord knows.

Paul also lost his comrade, Demas, to the things of the world. How heartbreaking for him! Yes, ministry is not for wimps. God will give peace and power to endure. It may sound trite when passing through the deep waters, but test God and, most of all, trust him.

Helps for Hurdlers

1. Realize that hurt could be a reality in your life of ministry. Ask God to prepare your heart. Soak up the following Scriptures: Psalm 23:1-6, 34:18, 55:22, 145:14,18; Isaiah 66:13; John 14:1; Romans 8:28; and 2 Corinthians 1:3-4.
2. Remind yourself that God has a plan for your life. Jeremiah 29:11 says, "For I know the plans I have for you…plans to prosper you and not harm you, plans to give you hope and a future." Keep your eyes on the finish line and not the hurdles. God is waiting for you there. Run to his arms.
3. Be transparent with your friend or prayer partner whom you know will keep your hurt in confidence and pray regarding all that happens to you.

4. Seek a biblical counselor as John did, if necessary, to help you through a difficult time.

5. You can cry but don't crumble. Jesus expressed "grief to the point of death" in the Garden of Gethsemane. Remember, however, he prayed, "Not my will but thine be done." God strengthened him. He said to the disciples when his betrayal was immanent, "Get up. Let's get going." (Matthew 26:36-46) Study and memorize verses that will help you get going and remind you from whom your strength comes. (Read Deuteronomy 31:6-8, Psalm 18:1-3, Isaiah 40:28-31, 2 Corinthians 1:7-10, and Philippians 4:13)

Discussion Questions for Teammates

1. How might you counsel Mary or John in their sad situations? Could they have been more discerning? Why or why not?

2. Read Jeremiah 9:4-5, 17:5-7, and Psalm 55:12-14. How can friendships and relationships in ministry be so fragile at times? What causes the confusion?

3. Read Micah 7:5, Psalm 41:9, 118:8-9, and 146:3. In what or whom are we not to trust? In whom are we to trust?

4. Share about a time when you felt misled or even betrayed by a comrade in ministry. How did you handle or mishandle the situation?

5. What do you do to help you make right choices in ministry?

HURDLE 7

Misunderstanding of Forgiveness – "I forgave. I'll be all right"

Andrew and his wife had eagerly trained and desired to serve the Lord through an overseas assignment. While happily ministering on the other side of the world, they received a call from the board of their worldwide mission organization. After much prayer and discernment, they obediently responded when the board asked Andrew to become the next president.

Andrew's expectation was to have a supportive, encouraging board. While he knew the board expected him to know and uphold the articles, by-laws, and other rules of the organization, he expected the board to do the same. What he increasingly discovered over the years was a board that would play favorites with some people, even when it meant ignoring the rules, disregarding and disrespecting him as president. His respect for the board and ability to work with them declined to the point that he felt it was only fair to all involved for him to step down.

Andrew felt a huge betrayal, questioning, "Why does it hurt more when it comes from people who should have your back?" He was willing to admit his own faults and lack of spiritual maturity may have contributed to or exacerbated the situation. However, the situation was never recognized by the board or addressed in any way.

Andrew knew he was clearly called to forgive because God's character is one of forgiveness, and we are created in God's image. He felt that forgiveness is not a feeling; it is an obedience that honors God. Many times, as an act of his will, he prayed to God to help him forgive.

He felt that hurt and disappointment are not always mutually expressed on both sides. Sometimes one party is oblivious to how it hurts another. Andrew was more than willing to forgive but realized that though he found the actions of the board to be offensive, he could still have ongoing friendships with board members outside of the boardroom. Although there are some members with whom he will never again enjoy close friendship, forgiveness has not failed.

For a few people forgiveness may be miraculously instantaneous, but most people find forgiveness a process that takes time and work with the goal of being able to pray God's best for people who have hurt them. In Matthew 18:21, Peter asked Jesus, "How many times should I forgive my brother who sins against me? Up to seven times?"

Jesus responded in verse 22, "I tell you, not seven times, but seventy-seven times"

His response indicates time and persistence. When we think we have forgiven someone and the devil brings up the offense again, we have the responsibility to keep forgiving. That indicates work! In time our heart will catch up with our responses, even if it is the 70th time. In the meantime, God will show us things about our heart that need his touch. It is not the number of times but the continual attitude of forgiveness that is necessary.

Cheryl, a pastor's wife, discovered that forgiveness for her was a daily process that she needed to work through with God's help. Her situation taught her that some hurt is intentional, for sure. However, most often the cause of the hurt is subtle and even confusing at times. Satan enjoys causing confusion and what better place than among God's servants. We are unaware of his schemes. (2 Cor. 2:5-11) He loves to make the church look like a group of hypocrites who can't get along with each other. He also enjoys maiming those in ministry to render them useless, cowering in defeat and self-pity.

Leadership Forum invited Cheryl, who also conducted a multi-faceted women's program in their church, to participate in a retreat for women whose husbands shepherded more than 1,000 people. She joyfully joined 25 other women in Colorado Springs at the Navigator headquarters, anticipating a weekend of sweet fellowship. She couldn't wait to glean as much as possible from the older, wiser wives. The Bible study and prayer times were spiritually rich. The Holy Spirit was working among them.

All seemed wonderful, but as the occasion allowed opportunity for transparent sharing among the women, Cheryl recalled, "My new friends opened their hearts, exposing deep wounds. I listened sympathetically as one woman after another shared how she was struggling emotionally due to hurts inflicted by believers in their churches. Staff had betrayed some of them and, in other instances, church members were the source of painful criticism and discouragement."

She tearfully wondered how that could be. Were their church members spiritually immature, undisciplined in their walk with the Lord? With this much hurt, how could the pastor couple continue their service?

Then Cheryl prayed, "Oh, God, please spare me from this kind of heart-breaking hurt as I serve in your Kingdom."

Several years passed and what about Cheryl? How did the Lord respond to her prayer? Has she survived the ministry years unscathed? "Certainly not! she says. "God has taught me valuable lessons of dependence on him, and with his help I learned to let go of a deep hurt that crashed into our lives."

A few decades ago, Cheryl's husband, with encouragement from some laymen in the community, started a church that grew to a regular attendance of more than 1,800 people. That church, in turn, started ten other churches, which likewise began other churches. Today the network includes more than 30 churches.

After faithfully loving and serving its members for almost three decades, Cheryl's husband, Curt, announced his impending retirement. He revealed to the church elders his transition plan, designed to prove smooth transition for everyone involved, including staff, elders, congregation, and incoming pastor. When the elders revealed a different plan, in submission to their leadership, he complied with their plan.

He had taught in leadership and new members' classes that congregations should have a vital role in the choosing of a new pastor. He felt that congregations should meet and hear the candidates after the selection committee's suggestions. The congregation, who has been praying, should be able to express its opinions and desires to the elders. Then the elders vote. However, the elders at Curt's church decided differently and left the congregation out of the process. They stood in front of the congregation on a Sunday morning and said, "Here is your new pastor."

Both plans, the elders' and Pastor Curt's, agreed that Curt and Cheryl would stay away from the church the first year after his retirement to allow the new leadership and congregation ample opportunity to adjust. Then they would return as members and serve in any way the leaders deemed necessary. Pastor Curt felt he had laid a secure, biblical foundation on which the new administration could build. Curt and Cheryl knew change was inevitable but were totally unprepared for what happened.

They left the state and committed not to listen to anyone's concerns, including friends and family who, in turn, kept silent about what was happening to the church. In desperation, ten months later friends began to share their concerns. Imagine their surprise when it became obvious that a wrecking ball was attacking all things that might stand as reminders of the thriving church they had left behind.

They kept quiet but prayed more diligently. At the conclusion of their year's absence, the elders and pastor sent them a letter inviting them to return to the church, however, with shocking stipulations on Curt. He was told he could possibly preach once a year at the discretion of the new pastor. He could not teach an adult class or be involved in any mission activity of the church, even though worldwide missions was his passion.

They never told Curt or Cheryl why those decisions were made. Curt and Cheryl decided it would be best not to return and face questions from church members as to why Curt was simply occupying a seat on Sunday morning. They wanted what was in the best interest of the church. Instead, he was invited to mentor one of the daughter church pastors, which became their excuse for not returning. Their older daughter and her family, who had tried to fit into the new scheme of things, felt uncomfortable and decided to attend another church. Their younger daughter and husband lived out of state and avoided having to make a painful decision regarding the church.

Friendships grew strained and Cheryl's heart broke as she ran into church members who asked questions she could not honestly answer. A few years have passed and many people, including most of the elders who made the transition decisions, have left the church. The mission budget dwindled. Very few of the staff members who worked with Curt remain at the church. Daughter churches were sadly neglected. However, several of them have grown larger than the mother church. The pastor that replaced Curt has left the church, and it is slowly returning to some of its original roots and beginning to grow again.

Two other churches in the area, after viewing what happened, asked a lot of questions and purposefully avoided the pitfalls when their pastors announced their impending retirements.

This has been a valley that Curt and Cheryl wouldn't wish on anyone. They have heard their story repeated occasionally by retiring pastors. At one point it still hurt to drive by the church. It has been grievous to see dear ones hurting, people to whom they ministered, especially those who invested time and resources in the church. However, the spiritual maturity of former church members allows them to grieve only long enough until they find other churches and avenues in which to exercise their spiritual gifts. Many of the church members now attend other churches in the area and have ministry roles. One pastor has personally thanked Curt for the mature Christians that his church has received with open arms.

One would think that the more than a thousand expressions of appreciation from their church members at the time of Curt's retirement would compensate for the hurt inflicted by a few. Trying not to dwell on the few, Cheryl daily perused an acrostic, F-O-R-G-I-V-E, that the Lord had given her to hold herself accountable for forgiveness. She readily shares it with us.

Face the past - Buried hurts yield unforgiveness and pain. When we admit that we have been hurt – intentionally or unintentionally – by non-Christian or Christian, we take the first step to begin the healing process of forgiveness.

Own the present - After admitting our hurt, we must realize the overwhelming necessity to forgive. We can say that God in his grace can help us forgive immediately and instantaneously, but for many of us it is a much longer process than we ever thought possible. However long the process, we must begin right now – no longer procrastinating, and stop the self-pity.

Read God's Word - Hebrews 4:12 informs us that God's Word *is living and active. Sharper than any double-edged sword…; it judges* *the thoughts and attitudes of the heart.* And 2 Timothy 3:6 reminds us that the *God-breathed Scripture is useful for teaching, rebuking, correcting, and training in righteousness.*

When we realize its incomparable, comprehensive ability not only to challenge but also to comfort, how can we not resist turning to God's Word for power when seeking to forgive?

Give praise - One's heart cannot focus on unforgiveness when it is full of praise. James R. Bishop wrote in *The Spirit of Christ in Human Relationships* about a farmer with a vengeful spirit who would seek to get even by throwing a dead cat into his neighbor's well. On one occasion the cat was washed out by the force of an overflowing artesian well. One whose heart is filled with the joy of the Lord is like that. Satan may attempt to inject bitterness and resentment, but the overflowing joy will keep the heart pure, the spirit sweet and clean.

Imitate Christ - Christ's words from the Cross, "Father, forgive them for they know not what they do," (Luke 23:34) have resounded loudly throughout the years and around the world. He who paid the ultimate sacrifice for our sins set the supreme example. Not only on the Cross but also at other times during his three years of ministry, Jesus demonstrated patience and forgiveness toward those who offended, denied, and betrayed him. As Ephesians 4:32 implies, we should, "Be kind and compassionate to one another, forgiving each other, just as in Christ God forgave you."

Voice the positive - How often are we tempted to speak negatively about someone who has hurt us? How often are we tempted to crawl under blankets of pity and depression when God would want us to throw off the blankets, crawl out of bed, get on our feet, and start thinking contentedly and positively about our situations. The possible worst-case scenario is never as difficult as we, in our negativity, would see it. When we begin to speak positively, we start to think and feel positively.

Examine my own motives - When we have been hurt, especially while ministering to others, we should always examine our own motives. How easily we could take little opportunities, knowingly or unknowingly, to even the score! Sometimes even facial expressions could reveal displeasure toward a person or group. We must ask God to give us pure hearts of forgiveness.

If we would ask Cheryl today about her work on forgiveness, she would tell us that she can honestly pray for those who hurt them. She no longer sighs when she drives by the church. A wise friend had reminded her that the church was not the building but the people in whose lives she and her husband had so lovingly invested. She often prays for God to bless it. She is focused on other ways to minister. Has she reached the 70 times count yet? She is not even concerned about that. God has been faithful!

She often thinks of the best lesson of forgiveness she learned as a child in a growing church. She remembers the spring morning her mother tenderly told her of her Sunday school teacher's sudden death. A drunk driver had crossed the median and smashed into her car while she was on her way home from a baby shower for a church member the previous evening. She was killed instantly, and her daughter, the mother of two small children, was critically injured. The drunk driver survived the crash with no injuries.

A few months previously, her teacher's husband, Art, a recovering alcoholic, had shared his testimony of having recently accepted Christ as his Savior. He and his wife started happily serving the Lord in the church. Cheryl wondered, "How will the accident affect Art? Will his daughter live? Will he be mad at God?"

Everyone sat in stark silence the Sunday evening following the accident when Art stood to share what God was teaching him as a result of the accident. One of the first things he did after making funeral arrangements for his wife was visit the man in jail who was responsible for his wife's death. He shared with him how Jesus Christ had transformed his own life. Granting the man forgiveness, Art realized that God had protected himself from causing a similar accident. The drunk driver, so stricken by Art's forgiveness and God's love, accepted Christ as his own personal Savior.

They buried Art's wife in the cemetery by the church. Frequently, Cheryl looked over at her teacher's grave and remembered the lesson of forgiveness that Art taught all of them. While working through the F-O-R-G-I-V-E acrostic, Cheryl often thought that if God could help Art face his hurt and forgive the man responsible for his wife's death, God could help anybody face past hurts and forgive.

Wounds and deep hurts take time to heal. And they leave scars. Our only hope is to forgive. If we choose not to, the results can cripple us emotionally, physically, and spiritually. Christ's words remind us, "For if you forgive men their sins, your Father will also forgive you. But if you do not forgive men their sins, your Father will not forgive your sins." (Matthew 6:14)

Corrie Ten Boom, a Dutch Christian, with her family hid Jews during the Nazi Holocaust. They spent time imprisoned in the horrible concentration camps for their efforts. After learning to forgive the people who inflicted the most horrific punishments, she talked about forgiveness. "If you have ever seen a country church with a bell in the steeple, you will remember that to get the bell ringing you have to tug on the rope awhile. Once it has begun to ring, you merely maintain the momentum. If you keep pulling, the bell keeps ringing. Forgiveness is letting go of the rope. It is just that simple." (azquotes.com)

Helps for Hurdlers

1. Know that your identity is not that of one who has been harmed but that of a beloved child of your Father in

heaven. God's love for you and his work in your life are not diminished. Take your eyes off the betrayer and remember the goodness of God. Read Scriptures that remind you of God's love for you. (Study Jeremiah 31:3, John 3:16, Romans 5:8, Ephesians 2:4-5, and 1 John 3:1.)

2. Read the following verses: Matthew 6:24, Mark 11:25, Ephesians 4:32, and Colossians 3:13. Ask God to help you forgive if you are struggling with your attitude towards a person or group of people.
3. Ask a trusted person to hold you accountable in the area of forgiveness. Ask him or her to check your attitude weekly.
4. Look for the lessons the Lord has for you in the process of forgiveness that might not be available anywhere else.
5. Daily work through the F-O-R-G-I-V-E acrostic.

Discussion Questions for Teammates

1. In addition to Jesus, name others in Scripture who forgave an offender. (Read Genesis 33:4, 45:12-15, 1 Samuel 24:1-22, and Acts 7:54-60.)
2. Is the wounded believer obligated to maintain silence for the overall good of Christendom? Why or why not?
3. Is it easier to forgive a non-Christian who lacks the same moral standards we proclaim? Why or why not?
4. Even if we have forgiven the offender, how do we manage emotionally when the offense continues to severely affect others whom we love?
5. Optional: Share about a time when you struggled with the process of forgiveness. How did it affect your ministry?

HURDLE 8

Wrong Priorities – "The work comes first. My family understands."

A Christian musician, Ed, was accompanying an evangelist, Frank, in a distant state for meetings in a large church. Frank mentioned that his son, whom he had not seen in months attended a college near the church where they were ministering. The afternoon before the first meeting, the son, Ryan, came to visit his father in the hotel suite Ed and Frank were sharing.

Ed noticed that Frank was busy catching up on emails and neglecting his son, so Ed tried to entertain him. After fifteen minutes, Ryan asked his dad a question. Frank, too occupied to listen to his son, didn't respond. Ryan stood up, started to leave, sadly looked at Ed and said, "What's the use?"

Noting that his son was gone, Frank looked at Ed and said, "What's a dad to do? He couldn't even stay long enough for a proper visit."

Sadly, Ryan didn't find any time that week to hear his dad preach.

Neglect of children in the ministry due to ministry pressures and wrong priorities has affected many young people throughout history. Missionary parents in remote areas have especially struggled with whether they should home school their children or send them away to boarding school. For some families boarding school has worked fine, depending largely on the quality of house parents caring for the children.

A well-known missionary kid, Thomas, told the trauma of being separated from his parents while they served in Asia. His grandparents took care of him in the United States. He suffered severe asthma, sometimes threatening his life.

While he attended a Christian college, the Lord confronted him about the bitterness that had taken root and grown in his heart toward his parents. He surrendered his bitterness to the Lord and sought his parents' forgiveness. He awakened a few years later to realize he had not had another asthma attack since he had resolved the bitterness. God helped Thomas and made him a stronger person as a result of his childhood.

One might ask, "Why did he have to be put in a position in the first place where he had to deal with bitterness? What about his parents' responsibility? What about the children who never deal with their bitterness?"

Those of us in ministry have no assurances that our children will not embarrass us or walk away from the Lord. Approximately 80% of pastors believe pastoral ministry has negatively affected their families. ("Statistics in the Ministry,", Pastoral Care, Inc., 2020) We must diligently pray for them and determinedly place our families as our number one priority aside from our own walks with the Lord.

We also can work on practical steps to keep our children out of the fishbowl and in the security blanket of our homes.

Many ministry parents fail to recognize the importance to *establish discipline*, including consequences, in our homes. Focused so much on ministry and facing ridicule, parents avoid the embarrassment of correcting their children in public. Children are smart enough to know how to take advantage of the situation. They realize it is safer to act out in public than in their own homes.

First Samuel 2:12-26 tells the sad story of Eli, the priest who failed to discipline his own sons who were desecrating the altar of God and blatantly living in sin. The consequences were costly, with God taking the lives of the sons and forbidding any more priests from Eli's lineage.

Pastor Justin and his family welcomed a missionary couple and their young son to their home for an evening meal during their church's weekend missionary conference. The primary speaker, staying at the pastor's home, was also included in the meal. When the adults were enjoying conversation after the meal, the young son slipped from his parents' view.

Suddenly, the child appeared, carrying and rummaging through the main speaker's billfold. Although the parents laughed and half-heartedly corrected the boy, his behavior the remaining weekend only became worse. While in the preschool class on Sunday morning, he established dominance when he didn't get to play with a toy he desired. He promptly dipped a cup in the toilet from the adjoining restroom and threw it on the teacher.

Another time undisciplined children hurt their parents' image was while the parents were interviewing at the mission's headquarters to become missionaries to South America. The children became upset with the very pregnant missionary wife who had volunteered to babysit them. After she had desperately tried to keep them from hitting one another, they, in turn, grabbed and threw billiard balls at her.

What actions, if any, were the church and missionary organization to take regarding the futures of these young couples? The church did not take support in one young couple, and the missionary organization accepted the other young couple for ministry overseas; however, their work was greatly hindered by the behavior of their children.

Contrast these stories with amazing stories of ministry children whose parents established boundaries and disciplined in love.

We must always *extend grace* and love to our children – quantity as well as quality times. Many people in ministry give the excuse for not spending quantity time with their children by saying, "I spend quality time with my children and that is what counts."

Ask the child whose dad or mom misses a birthday, an important sporting event or concert. Ask the child whose dad is never home in the evening to read a book, help with homework, eat a meal, or tuck her or him in bed.

Pastor Ron had one compelling desire in ministry. He prayed he would never see the day his two daughters would ever accuse him of neglecting them. Every Saturday morning, he would take one of his daughters to a local restaurant of her choice for a father-daughter date. He alternated weeks with the girls so he could give each one his undivided attention. He also noted and attended their school and sporting events on his calendar.

His determination and discipline paid off. Years later, when his girls were in college, he listened to them share in a class on parenting, being taught by him and his wife. The girls brought tears to their parents' eyes when they shared, "We have always felt loved. We never heard our parents raise their voices in anger to each other."

Pastor Ron's girls grew up to marry godly young men who became the spiritual leaders of their homes, which comforted Ron and his wife to know their grandchildren were in Christian homes.

Ron indeed was especially blessed the evening he had the joy of baptizing his two oldest grandsons.

Were Ron's children perfect? By no means, but they understood the grace extended to them and love wrapped around them.

Another step that ministry parents could do to protect our children is to *exercise discretion*. Pastor Caleb desired to protect his wife and children from situations in the church that they couldn't help. Of course, his wife, Isabella would pray, but he shielded her. Unless the ministry she worked in included a church member under discipline, she didn't know about the situation.

Children do not need to be involved or burdened with heavy and heartbreaking situations. If parents are fighting unforgiveness and bitterness toward church members who are causing trouble, children do not need to be negatively influenced. Children, who are vulnerable, need to be reminded more of the blessings than the burdens. "It would be better for him to be thrown into the sea with a millstone tied around his neck than for him to cause one of these little ones to sin." (Luke 17:2)

As people in ministry, we also need to *educate our congregations or teams* about our priorities for our families. It is reported that 35% of pastors report the demands of the church denies them from spending time with their family. ("Statistics in the Ministry," Pastoral Care Inc., 2020) It would be prudent for the pastoral family to set the example for other families in the congregation.

Pastor Joshua interviewed for the lead pastor position in a church in another state. He decided to only interview if all his family members agreed. After all, the following year was going to be his daughter's senior year of high school. When they all agreed he should interview, he told the search committee that although he would serve the church to the best of his ability, his family's needs would be his top priority. The search committee, thrilled with his response, had already sought references and knew that putting his family first had always been his practice, only strengthening his overall ministry.

Pastor Joshua also made it a practice to not run always whenever someone declared an emergency. He truly knew what constituted an emergency, and some situations had been a long time in the process. Those involved, though, sometimes thought every step along the way was an emergency.

Jill, a pastor's wife, enjoyed watching her daughter participate in the youth activities of the church. The leaders of the youth ministry had decided to present a program to the whole church. The students were told that they would need to audition for the various parts. Jill's daughter, Kaitlyn, practiced and practiced, wanting one specific part. Jill listened to her tryout and knew in her heart that Kaitlyn would be perfect for the part.

However, Kaitlyn came home one evening very discouraged because she didn't get the part. One of the youth workers caught Jill in the hallways of church the next Sunday saying, "I hope Kaitlyn is okay with not getting picked for the part she wanted. I figured because she was the pastor's daughter, she could handle disappointment better than the other students."

Jill gently and quietly educated the youth worker, "Kaitlyn, in this instance, is not the pastor's daughter but an average kid in the youth group with feelings just like all the others in the group. She will eventually get over the rejection, not because she is the pastor's daughter but because she is a forgiving Christian."

How many times in our ministries are we guilty of pressuring our children to be perfect? We pick all kinds of battles with them when we should eliminate unnecessary battles that really aren't that important in the grand scheme. We need to pray for discernment when choosing battles.

When Pastor Sam and Chloe's sweet, kind teenage daughter came home from the store with a decent but shorter skirt than they preferred, they chose not to make a big deal out of her purchase. Instead, they agreed to watch her behavior to see if her other items of clothing became lax or seductive. The daughter was happy with her skirt to help her identify with her friends; yet, she alone put limits on the other items of clothing.

We wonder how she would have responded if Sam and Chloe had needlessly punished her, making a big deal out of a decent but short skirt. By the way, the daughter is in ministry today.

Lastly, we must all realize the importance of spouses in ministry. After the children are gone from the home and those of us in ministry retire, we hopefully will still have our spouses, who have been faithful and loving supports through all the ministry years. When those times come, we will also have friends and memories of fruitful times for which to thank and praise the Lord.

In conclusion, Pastor Carl wanted to share with us about his family and ministry, "For many years my responsibilities as a pastor took priority over my family. I gave my wife much of my own parental duties. This was especially true regarding my son. After repenting of my neglect, I wrote a letter to my son, asking for his forgiveness. My letter greatly helped with the good relationship we have today."

Helps for Hurdlers

1. Think about times you may have placed ministry before your family. What were the results?
2. Be willing to repent if you have neglected your children for ministry. Humble yourself and ask for their forgiveness.
3. Evaluate boundaries you have established to protect your family. Do they need to be changed or updated as your children have grown?
4. Plan a special vacation for your family. Pray God will provide resources. However, remember time away together does not have to be lavish. It may take scheduling around all the activities in which the children are involved but do it anyway.
5. Constantly tell your family that you love them. If it feels awkward at first, do it anyway. One 40-year-old man cried when he heard his father say he loved him for the first time.

_SPECIFIC

Charles and Vicki Lake

Discussion Questions for Teammates

1. Name families in Scripture who are both good and bad examples of families.
2. Read 1 Samuel 2:12-36. What do you think caused Eli's sons to be so rebellious and disobedient? What happened to them?
3. Read John 19:25-27. How did Jesus feel about his mother during his dying moments? We so often talk about caring for our children, but who of us still have parents alive, and what are our responsibilities to them during our days of ministry?
4. Discuss the qualifications for a church leader in 1 Timothy 3:1-7. What part do families play? Discuss leaders in your church or ministry who "manage their families well."
5. Share the joys and concerns you have for your families. Commit to pray regularly for the spouses and children of your staff or team.

HURDLE 9

A Need to Impress – "It's got to be big or it's no good."

In a small church in a small town in Eastern Kentucky, Pop Franklin, a foreman at a local steel mill, taught a small Sunday School class of small boys. Although the boys had experienced other teachers who faithfully taught them the Bible, Pop took over the class when the boys were approximately ten years old. At the end of the year when the boys were to be promoted to another teacher, Pop announced he was going to promote himself with his boys. He eventually taught the boys for most of their growing years through high school graduation. He not only instilled Scripture in their minds and hearts but also took advantage of fishing and camping trips to teach the boys valuable life lessons.

Is it any surprise that when the boys matured physically and spiritually, they became leaders in the community with several of them going into full-time ministry? Two of them became plant managers at the town's two largest businesses, an oil refinery and a steel plant. Another one of the young boys later served as a minister-at-large for a worldwide mission organization as well as pastored two churches with worldwide impacts. Pop also greatly influenced his younger brother-in-law who became a missionary and pastor as well as his son-in-law who became a pastor and biblical counselor.

A few years ago, the small church decided to remodel the sanctuary. When one of Pop's relatives heard that the church was going to tear out the original wooden altar at the front of the platform, he asked if he could have the railing. He decided to cut it into smaller altars, refinish the wood, and give the portions to men who had been influenced by Pop.

Does one have to have a big ministry to have a big impact? One only needs to be obedient to God's call and let God take care of the bigness.

Philip is probably one of the best examples of obeying God's call to minister to the "one." During a joyful revival in Samaria, where many were turning to Christ, God sent an angel to Philip. "Now an angel of the Lord said to Philip, 'Go south to the road – the desert road – that goes down from Jerusalem to Gaza.'" (Acts 8:26)

Without question, Philip obeyed and along the road he met an Ethiopian official who was reading and trying to understand a passage in Isaiah. At the right time and place, Philip explained the Scriptures to the Ethiopian who accepted Christ and asked Philip to baptize him.

It is doubtful that any person in ministry has not been guilty, at some time or another, of playing the comparison game. We compare our gifts with others we feel are more gifted, the size of our ministry with the size of others who have been at it for a much longer time, and even our appearance as we see those more blessed than we perceive ourselves to be.

We grow less content with ourselves as we see the multiplying resources for ministry created by celebrity pastors of mega-churches, articles about churches meeting in multiple sights, and conferences that are directed toward pastors and workers in the larger churches of our country.

The Bible is full of illustrations of those who played the game. For example, Moses said to the Lord, "Oh Lord, I have never been eloquent neither in the past nor since you have spoken to your servant. I am slow of speech and tongue." (Exodus 4:10)

Playing the game can make it easy for us to fall prey to jealousy, envy, discouragement and even depression. Most discouraging is when we start to compare our spiritual gifts with the gifts of others. Paul best stated the caution in 2 Corinthians 10:12, "We do not dare to classify or compare ourselves with some who commend themselves. When they measure themselves by themselves and compare themselves with themselves, they are not wise."

He further commented, "Let him who boasts boast in the Lord. For it is not the one who commends himself who is approved, but the one whom the Lord commends." (2 Corinthians 10:17-18)

Paul also knew his limitations. "When I came to you, brothers, I did not come with eloquence or superior wisdom as I proclaimed to you the testimony of God. I came to you in weakness and fear, and with much trembling. My message and my preaching were not with wise and persuasive words, but with a demonstration of the Spirit's power, so that your faith might not rest on men's wisdom but on God's power." (1 Corinthians 2:1-5)

Too many pastors might be guilty of seeking to build their large congregations while overlooking the one individual. Pastor Ken was on the staff of a large congregation where many people attended multiple services. He didn't have too many responsibilities at the Saturday evening service, so he tried to interact with people as they came for church. He soon noticed an older gentleman who came with his daughter and her family. Buddy had recently lost his wife and had moved to live with his daughter.

Buddy knew no one at the church other than his family and

often ended up sitting in a chair in the lobby, waiting for them to finish talking with their friends. He looked lonely so one Saturday evening Pastor Ken sat in a chair with a side table separating the two of them. Buddy would simply smile at Pastor Ken the following weeks when he sat next to him. Pastor Ken said, "It just seemed right to sit next to the guy as he waited."

Eventually, he asked Pastor Ken, "Why do you always sit with me?"

That was the start of a super fun friendship. They discovered they both liked corny jokes, which kept Pastor Ken busily trying to find a joke for his Saturday evening encounter. After two years of sitting and telling jokes with one another, Pastor Ken and his family moved to another church in another community. Occasionally, Buddy's daughter would send Pastor Ken a note, "Dad sure misses you."

And then the phone call came, "Dad passed away."

Pastor Ken went to his funeral which was held in a little, country church because the big church didn't have space for his service. Eight people besides family members attended his funeral. As Pastor Ken left the service, Buddy's daughter gave him a prized possession which now sits in his office. It was Buddy's signature cap to serve as a reminder of the small ministries with big impacts.

No matter the size of the church, it is comprised of individuals to whom we must minister in the most effective ways possible, and we must do it with accountability.

Pastor Robert made it clear that if he were to accept the call to a certain church, he was not to be accountable to anyone. He would only run a staff-driven church. Eager for his exceptional preaching at the time, the search committee granted the young pastor his wish. Years passed and he built what many would consider to be a mega church. He became a celebrity pastor in his denomination and often boasted of his friendships with important people. He made all the decisions, the hiring and even firing of any staff members who slightly disagreed with him.

The church campus was big and impressive. However, something became apparently wrong as numbers started dwindling, no one responded to invitations at the conclusion of the services, and giving decreased. When Pastor Robert was challenged, things grew worse and he left suddenly, leaving the church in a mess. Accusations flew and members also left. The church members loved their pastor but were left with questions. The young staff who had never been trained for such huge responsibilities depended heavily upon the Lord and did the best they could to hold the church together until they could find a new, qualified pastor. For them, big was no longer better.

Interestingly, most of the members who left Pastor Robert's large church are now attending and serving in smaller churches in the community. Those who minister in small churches and ministries also must realize their value. Today workshops, often at large conferences, provide encouragement and discussion for small ministries and churches.

Statistics from recent research by Ed Stetzer and Christian Schwartz tell us that ten smaller churches of 100 people will accomplish much more than one church of 1,000. Karl Vaters in a commentary in Leadership Journal, April 13, 2015, wrote, "Big and mega churches are great. And they get almost all the press, both positive and negative. They deserve our prayers and support, not second guessing, jealousy, and ridicule."

However, a sense of *security* exists for some pastors in small churches who would not function well in large church settings. We enjoy knowing every member in our congregations by name. Many church members also find security and satisfaction in their smaller churches. People who would be shy in leadership positions in large churches feel more comfortable serving in their smaller settings.

Smaller churches are more appropriate for some *settings*. Perhaps, they are in rural settings that would never draw large numbers. Yet the people in the community, especially farmers, need to grow in their relationships with the Lord and one another. Christians need intimate fellowship, whether it be in a smaller group within a large church or a smaller church setting.

A *smallness mindset* towards ministry is all that can be accomplished in many countries of the world where only small gatherings or house churches are permitted. Yet, in those house churches believers are strengthened and grow in fellowship. Missionaries have testified that they often feel the Lord's presence more in the small house churches than in some larger churches in other countries. The house churches do grow and start other house churches, so the church is being multiplied around the world.

Pastor Jonathon in the Midwest studied the effects of mega church ministry and decided that a church of 2,000 people would be more than he could adequately handle, even with sufficient staff. Thus, he felt a positive alternative was to plant daughter congregations which could expand the kingdom faster. At one time, for example, 250 people left Pastor Jonathon's church on a Sunday morning with his blessing and excitement. His congregation started ten churches which, in turn, started churches which, in turn, started churches and today they number more than 30 congregations.

Alex attended a small Christian college and befriended a group of guys, all of whom were preparing for the ministry. Although he felt at home with the group, he also felt out of place because he could never see himself standing before a group of people ministering the Word and pastoring a church.

After several years of discontent, he attended a family camp where He sensed God gently nudging him into ministry in the church. He realized that he needed to quit looking at himself and what he perceived to be his limitations and let God guide him to where he wanted him to be. It was God's choice, not his.

Soon after the camp, the Lord opened doors for him to fill the pulpit of a couple of small country churches who were without a pastor. He was shocked by the people's positive responses and found that his weekly preparations were becoming the joy of his life. Accompanied by a musically gifted wife, he began to see visible fruit from his ministry.

His call was to smaller, struggling churches. Never distracted by the ministry of the larger churches in the communities he served, he saw smaller churches come to life and have a vital outreach, both locally and around the world. Members of his congregations grew exponentially as he stressed daily discipleship and embraced a world in need.

Whether a ministry is small or large, it should never feel inferior or superior because of size. We all work together to fulfill the Great Commission. When we give account for our lives to the Lord Almighty, he won't ask us how big our church was. He'll want to know if we know him personally and was faithful to his call on our lives.

Helps for Hurdlers

1. Read 1 Corinthians 2:1-5 and 2 Corinthians 10:12. Examine yourself to see if you've fallen into the comparison trap of ministry.
2. Read 1 Corinthians 12. Know your purpose in ministry.
3. Keep your eyes focused on Christ (Hebrews 12:2) and his call on your life.
4. Write down ways, like Pastor Ken, that the Lord has encouraged your heart through ministry to one person.
5. Think of the sizes of the churches where you have experienced the most spiritual growth.

Discussion Questions for Teammates

1. Read Acts 8. Share about a time in your ministry when God led you to change from something you considered "successful" to something he deemed "special."
2. Share about any Pop Franklins in your life.

3. How can you help your team be more ministry-focused instead of numbers-focused, allowing God to take care of the numbers?
4. Share with your teammates about smaller ministries that have impacted you.
5. Read 1 Corinthians 12. What does the passage mean to you? Pray together that God will help your staff or team keep focused on God's unique ministry for each of you considering God's ministry for the entire church.

HURDLE 10

Fear of Fun – "This is no laughing matter."

We all know about Jack and Jill and their difficulties with hill climbing, but most of us do not know what became of the hapless pair as adults. The time has come to find out. Both went into Christian ministry. Jack was a senior pastor of a downtown, middle-sized church while Jill coordinated everything that went on for the children and teenagers of a giant, big-box, suburban church.

True story? There is no way to prove it, we admit. On the other hand, neither is there proof that they didn't pursue careers in ministry, so let's go with the assumption and see where it takes us.

Somewhere along in his pastoral preparations, Jack fell in with a group who held the view that because of the sacredness of their calling, they must wear dark suits, white shirts, and conservative ties and maintain solemn, earnest, concerned faces at all times, which meant that Jack was the center of grateful attention at funerals, but not at all popular at wedding receptions. A sense of humor was excess baggage for Pastor Jack.

Jill, however, sprang from a different root. No one told her that God prefers unrelenting solemnity. Neither had she heard that an active sense of humor is detrimental to one's spiritual leadership. So, whenever she saw the funny side of whatever confronted her at the moment, those around her were usually met by cheerful laughter. And if laughter was totally inappropriate, her eyes sparkled anyway. And she drew to herself the children to whom she ministered and their parents, like hungry bees swarming around purple clover, which smoothed paths and opened doors, making her job so much easier.

Some men and women like Jack have been told that those in ministry, whatever that ministry might be, should conduct themselves with all due regard for the holiness of God and the seriousness of their position. Holiness and respect are a crucial part of the mix, but do holiness and respect require total solemnity, with no laughter allowed? And how does such demeanor affect those whom they seek to lead?

Sometimes we take ourselves too seriously. If we could only learn to laugh at ourselves in awkward situations, we would genuinely enjoy ministry so much more. Pastors could write volumes about funny things that have happened to them in ministry. One of the funniest stories was when Justin, a youth pastor, who enjoyed making people laugh, became the one with laughter focused on him when he conducted his first funeral. He was trying extremely hard to be dignified and had achieved his goal, that is, until a car ran a stoplight and broadsided the hearse in which he was riding to the cemetery. Have you ever seen a funeral procession hit the curb and wait for another hearse to retrieve the remains and carry on? Justin could not wait to get back to the church to tell his view of the ordeal.

Of course, he made everyone laugh, saying there was one dead at the scene of the accident.

And speaking of funerals, Pastor Paul recently told of an unsacred moment as he spoke at the graveside of one of his church members. Being very bald, Paul had worn a lovely woolen cap to keep his head warm as the winter gusts blew across the cemetery. One gust quickly grabbed his cap and placed it in – you guessed it – the grave. Not wanting to see the pastor's cap buried beneath the casket, the funeral director quickly crawled down to rescue it. Picture that.

Those who know still laugh about the time that Paulette, a pastor's wife, accidently locked herself in the Alzheimer's Unit in a local nursing home at midnight. She had waited with her husband for the mortuary to pick up the body of his administrative assistant's mother who had just died. The pastor sent his wife to retrieve the car in the front parking lot while he helped take the body to the back door of the facility. Sleepily, she turned down the wrong hallway and heard the door click behind her. When she turned around and noticed the keypad by the locked doors, she knew instantly that she was locked in the Alzheimer's Unit.

Paulette repeatedly knocked on the window in the door to get the nurses' attention. Thinking that it was probably one of the residents wanting to escape the ward, they continued working with their papers and did not even glance Paulette's way. When the cleaning man who was mopping the hallways rounded the corner, she went into action. He noticed her and not recognizing her as a patient, notified the nurses at the station. They finally looked at her and they all laughed.

About the time they released Paulette, her husband approached. When he asked her where she had been, she promptly told him, "I don't think you could begin to guess."

The pastor's administrative assistant soon heard about Paulette's midnight adventure at the nursing home. At the viewing for her mother, she laughingly told Paulette, "When I heard about your escapades in the Alzheimer's Unit, I knew then that I could laugh again after losing my mom."

Those who have ministered through drama and music have many funny stories to share. Theresa will never forget the Saturday morning dress rehearsals when she directed the church's drama portion for the seasonal musicals. One Saturday morning she wanted to cry when the sweet lamb she had secured for the church's Easter musical did a number on the platform in front of the choir and drama team. Her assistant reluctantly gathered the stage crew and cleaned up the mess because Theresa had the good sense to stay in the balcony sound booth while the cleaning crew did their job.

Rather than follow the script and mourn over their failures during Jesus' crucifixion, five actors playing disciples in a boat pulled out a cell phone and faked a call to McDonalds to order lunch. It was the comic relief they all needed during the tense rehearsal.

The audience could not contain their laughter during a Christmas presentation at a small Midwestern church when choir members tented their music folders over their heads. A flying angel, strung up on a pulley wire, had become sick from too much swinging and started vomiting.

Nursery workers could write volumes about funny things that happen in the church nursery. One of the most-dramatic-at-the-time-but-funny-afterwards events was when one nursery worker panicked as a toddler took out his eyeball and rolled it across the floor. The parents, who were new to the church, had forgotten to inform the workers about the child's artificial eye. "Oh, yeah," they said, "we have been trying to break him of the habit of wanting to play with his artificial eyeball. It's a convenient toy for him."

And what about those who work in ministry offices? They are the first to see the notorious "church bloopers." While Susan was senior editor for a missionary organization, she learned to laugh at her mistakes. She and her assistant editor had little, furry giggle balls that they threw towards one another when stressed with deadlines. Susan's was red and her assistant's blue. When the ball hit the floor or wall, the fur flew, and the giggles rolled. Even the graphic designer down the hall could hear the giggles. Once when Susan wrote a small piece for some men associated with the organization, she had men "sinning" instead of "winning." That called for a giggle ball pitch.

Do you ever wonder what lighthearted moments occurred with Jesus and the disciples? Were they like brothers kidding one another? Which disciple or disciples took the brunt of some of the jokes? Thomas? Peter? Or John, the Beloved?

In the heaviness of ministry, we must learn to lighten the load with laughter. Throw a few giggle balls. Laugh at ourselves. Laugh with others. Lighten the load. Even King Solomon knew what is good for us. In Proverbs 17:22 (KJV) he wrote, "A merry heart doeth good like a medicine." We need a frequent dose of that remedy. The Bible says so.

Helps for Hurdling

1. Read a few Psalms regarding praise to lift your hearts upward. (Psalms 8, 9, 18, 19, 29, 33, 34, 46, 47, 48, 63, 66, 89, 92, 93, 95, 96, 98, 100, 103, 104, 105, 108, 111, 113, 117, 134, 135, 136, 139, 145, 146, 147, 148, 149, and 150)
2. Learn to laugh at yourself. Perhaps, something that you thought was a dire necessity turns out to be a laughing matter instead.
3. Ask the Lord to show you fun stories or Facebook posts to lighten your soul.
4. Ask the Lord to give you a funny friend, one who will make you laugh whenever you talk to her or him.
5. Frequently recall the funny stories in your ministry to not take yourself too seriously.

Questions for Discussion

1. Study the following biblical passages: Ecclesiastes 3:4 and Proverbs 15:13, 30. What are your thoughts regarding the passages?
2. Study John 16:33. Why should Christians, more than others, have cause to rejoice?
3. Paul E. McGhee, Ph.D., writes, "Your sense of humor is one of the most powerful tools you have to make certain that your daily mood and emotional state support good health." And health personnel are now claiming that laughter does benefit the body. In fact, a Mayo Clinic quote says, "Laughter is powerful, stress-relief medicine." How, then, can laughter specifically help us in ministry?
4. Share about someone you know in ministry who is effective with light-heartedness.
5. Share some funny things that have happened to you in ministry.

Conclusion

We shared only a portion of the stories that ministers and missionaries willingly sent to us. With the stories came resounding encouragement to finish the book. Well, we have reached the finish line for them as well as for those in ministry who, hopefully, will accept the challenge to victoriously fly over the hurdles set before them.

Our purpose from the start was to keep people in ministry from stumbling over any hurdles facing them in ministry. We have also thought of all the laypeople, volunteering to run alongside and often flying over some of the same hurdles. We remind you that clipping or even knocking over a hurdle, unless intentionally done so, will not disqualify you from the race. Keep on hurdling.

Hurdles' rules state that only those who have two false starts or try to cheat when going over a hurdle will disqualify themselves. Remember, too, that stumbling does not disqualify you. You can pick yourself up and finish the race. And, what if you get injured? You may need some time for healing. Sabbaticals are helpful in giving the minister a time for rest and recharging. Furloughs for missionaries serve the same purpose, except missionaries are often challenged with fund raising, too. Retreat centers are available with minimal charges for those in ministry. (Pastor Retreat Centers, my-pastor.com) Never be ashamed to see a biblical counselor, as well.

The best hurdlers are the ones who train hard and are flexible. Ministry is not for wimps! What we experience in a ministry setting may not be what we expected. That's where patience, perseverance, and flexibility go a long way in helping us finish the race.

May we remind you that you are never alone when flying over the hurdles. The Holy Spirit, our Advocate, is the one who indwells and enables us to minister. He is also the Comforter, who is there to help us when we stumble.

We are also in the grandstands, praying and cheering for you as you keep your eyes focused on the goal. "Therefore, since we are surrounded by such a great cloud of witnesses, let us throw off everything that hinders and the sin that so easily entangles. And let us run with perseverance the race marked out for us, fixing our eyes on Jesus, the pioneer and perfecter of faith." (Hebrews 12:1-2a)

Now our charge to you is, "Go fly high through the race to which God has called you. You are most blessed to be a member of his team!"

About the Authors

Charles has pastored or served as a missionary since he was sixteen years old. He helped start Community Church of Greenwood in the Indianapolis area and served as senior pastor for 28 years until his retirement. While he was the pastor, the church planted ten daughter churches, and today third and fourth generation churches number 34 congregations in the U.S. and Brazil, South America. The church's annual budget for missions exceeded $600,000, and the network of churches gave more than $1.4 million the last year he served as pastor.

Since his retirement he has served four interim pastorates in Florida, Georgia, and Indiana. He also worked for five years for a church consulting firm and served as a consultant for discipleship for the Salvation Army.

Charles has served as adjunct professor for Trinity Evangelical Divinity School, Bethel University Graduate School in Indiana, Anderson School of Theology, West Africa Theological Seminary in Nigeria, and Emmaus Biblical Seminary in Haiti.

He has also served on the board of many Christian and civic organizations. He presently serves on the board of Emmaus Biblical Seminary in Haiti, where Growth Ministries of which he is the Director, has a vital discipleship ministry with MP3 players, especially targeting literacy-challenged believers.

Charles has written and published discipleship materials through Growth Ministries, *Worship Is* through Westbow Press; *Holy is a Four-Letter Word*, co-authored with Dr. Matt Ayars, through Wipf and Stock Publishers; and discipleship materials through the Salvation Army.

Charles earned an AB degree from Asbury University (formerly College), an MA degree from Butler University, and an MDiv degree and DMin degree from Asbury Theological Seminary.

Charles has traveled and spoken in more than 35 countries. He and Vicki also ministered one year in Australia.

Vicki's BA degree in English/Education from Anderson University (IN) and MA degree in Journalism from Ball State University have spurred her creativity in various editorial positions, including *Outreach* magazine for One Mission Society (formerly OMS International).

While leading the Potpourri Players at her church, Vicki wrote and directed full-length dramas, numerous vignettes, video scripts, and a radio series called *The Family Tree*. She also wrote vignettes for Chapel of the Air's *50-Day Adventure*.

Her published books are *Firming Up Your Flabby Faith* (James), Scripture Press' Women's Inductive Bible Studies; *Restored in the Ruins* (Nehemiah), Scripture Press' Tapestry Collection; *Absolutely! Can We Know What's Right and Wrong?* (based on John 13-15 and co-authored with Carroll Ferguson Hunt), Zondervan; and *Miraculous Movings of God – Celebrating 100 Years of Harvest*, One Mission Society (formerly OMS International).

Before their daughters were born, Vicki taught high school English and journalism. Later she served as an adjunct professor, teaching Communications for I.U. Kelley School of Business (Indianapolis campus).

Vicki has taught Bible studies to women at a unique Bible study/workshop format called Creative Patterns and at a Bible study for working women in downtown Indianapolis. Her love for ministry to women eventually led to directing the women's ministry of her church.

Vicki has also spoken to women's groups, given communication workshops, and presented a workshop at the Evangelical Press Association. Although she has traveled to more than 25 countries, her speaking highlight was sharing God's Word with women in Cuba.

Charles and Vicki have two married daughters, Kim (Chris), and Kara (Paul); three grandsons, Kyle, Cole, and Luke; and one granddaughter, Evelyn.

Printed in the United States
By Bookmasters